Edited by Laurie Anne Witwer

Printed in Canada

Published by Wordstorm Productions Inc.

Canadian Cataloguing in Publication Data

Rose, Perry P. (Perry Paul), 1948 -
Tales from the police locker room Vol 2
originally published under title: Blue-pers
ISBN 0-9697756-5-2 (v. 1) --- ISBN 0-9697756-6-0 (v. 2)

1. Police--Anecdotes. 2. Police--Humour.
I. Nelson, Joan, 1939- II. Title
III. Title: Blue-pers
PN6231.P59R69 1996   363.2'0202
C96-910715-3

For information contact:

WORDSTORM PRODUCTIONS INC.,
P.O. BOX 49132,
7740 - 18 STREET S.E.,
CALGARY, ALBERTA,
CANADA T2C 3W5
Email: wordstrm @cadvision.com

or

WORDSTORM PRODUCTIONS INC.,
1520 - 3rd ST NW, C104,
GREAT FALLS, MT USA 59404

Tales from the Police Locker room Vol. II

PErry p.rose

For information contact:

**WORDSTORM PRODUCTIONS
INC.,
P.O. BOX 49132,
7740 - 18 STREET S.E.,
CALGARY, ALBERTA,
CANADA T2C 3W5**
or

**WORDSTORM PRODUCTIONS INC.,
1520 - 3rd ST NW, BOX C104,
GREAT FALLS, MT USA 59404**

Art copyright © Perry P. Rose 1995

Cover Art © Perry P. Rose 1995

Edited by Laurie A. Witwer
Rose, Perry P., 1948-
ISBN 0-9697756-2-8
Printed in Canada
Published by Wordstorm Productions Inc.
First printing October 1995
Second printing November 1996

Other books by Perry P. Rose

TALES FROM THE POLICE LOCKER
ROOM Vol 1
(with Joan Nelson)
ISBN 0-9697756-0-1

FAXABLE LAUGHS - VOLUME 1
ISBN 0-9697756-1-X

To my brothers and sisters

INTRODUCTION

It really was a dark and stormy night. The call - a silent intruder alarm at a residence. The car crew ghosted to a stop a few doors away, engine off, lights out. Heavy rain danced on the hood of the blue and white patrol car sending showers of glistening droplets into the air under the glow of a single street lamp. The two protectors donned their hats, in case an inspector was lurking in the bushes, and quietly slid into the downpour.

With maglites in hand and nylon raincoats swishing, "sweee, swee, swee," they cautiously approached the residence in question.

"1234 to Dispatch, the front checks secure. Do we have a keyholder attending?" one of the constables asked quietly into his portable radio.

"10-4, we do," came the muffled reply as he put his hand over the speaker to keep the volume down. "Should be there in twenty minutes or so."

"Dispatch, we're not going to stand in this rain that long to wait. We'll check the rest of the perimeter and if nothing is disturbed we'll come back when the keyholder gets here."

"10-4, 1234."

"I'll stay at the front," he whispered to his younger and less experienced partner. "You zip around back and check things out."

"Okay," came the reply as the rookie bolted for the side gate, eager for the catch if there was to be one.

When he pulled on the handle he discovered that the wire mesh gate was locked. Drawing on all his recent physical training at the Academy he grasped the top of the fence, swung his legs high, and attempted to vault the obstacle. A combination of the lightening flash, the wet gate and the twenty-two pounds of equipment on his belt, caused him to

9

misjudge the height and he straddled the mesh. With a resounding rattle he settled very heavily onto the top support bar. The pain was excruciating.

"Are you okay?" came his partner's voice from the front of the house.

"Yeah," he grunted, lowering himself gently into the yard, "I think I just had a close encounter with Bobbit!"

His partner mumbled something indiscernible.

The house checked secure and the two very wet policemen carried on with their patrol.

The following day a call was received at the district office.

"City Police, how can I help you?"

"I would like to speak with Constable Dork, please," the caller stated.

"We have some dorks working here, but we don't have a Constable Dork," he replied.

"I'm sure you do, and I need to speak with him," the caller insisted.

The constable taking the call was puzzled, but in the name of customer service and sheer curiosity, he pressed.

"Maybe if you tell me what this is all about I can be of more assistance."

"That's easy, officer," she stated matter-of-factly, "Last night I had an alarm at my house while I was out. Two of your officers came by and checked around. My neighbour heard some thrashing about and opened her window to see what was going on. She heard one of the officers say to the other, 'Thirteen hundred partners to choose from and I get stuck with Constable Dork!' That's the guy I need to talk to."

Well, here I am back at it again! I'll bet you thought when you read my first book I must have told you every funny police story in the world. Wrong! You see the great thing about this is these bloopers continue to happen every day. I mean, where would we be without K-9 dogs that wouldn't, cars that didn't, drunks that couldn't and equipment that doesn't?

The rule of thumb I seem to have discovered in my search for stories is this: The more serious your job, the worse chance you have of making a complete fool of yourself. Like the inspector who had been off the street for a lengthy period of time and had a longing to return to the excitement of the chase and the thrill of the catch. He was following a car when he observed it signal and make a turn ahead of him. There was a sign, plain as could be, "NO LEFT TURN." He slid the police car in behind the suspect with a grin as he knew he was about to write his first ticket in a long time. A feeling of reward flooded over him as he stepped from his car, summons folder in hand.

"May I see your licence please," he said to the driver.

"What for?" the guy asked, rummaging around in his pocket for his wallet.

"You're being stopped for making an illegal left turn," the inspector replied.

"But I didn't make an illegal left turn," the man insisted.

"Yes you did," the inspector retorted, enjoying the forgotten argument at the side of the road. "I was right behind you when you made it."

"That was a *right* turn, not a *left* turn," the man complained.

Suddenly reality hit the inspector and his heart sank. He had read the sign wrong. However, not wanting to lose his ground, he reached into his pocket and pulled out his car keyring. On it was a safe driving medallion he had received from the Traffic Section the year before during a safe driving campaign. He slipped it from his keyring and passed it to the driver.

"You're absolutely correct, sir," he said with a smile. "This was a test and you proved to me that you really are paying attention to the rules of the road. On behalf of the Police Department I would like to present you with this Safe Driving Award. Display it with pride!"

Or how about the young motorcycle cop who thought he looked really cool on his Harley with a white silk scarf blowing out behind him. He thrilled at the feeling of the silk on his neck and the flutter of it behind his ears as he rode. One fine day he was driving in the downtown core at lunch time when hundreds of people were out on the sidewalks. He approached a corner and grinned to himself as the crowd waited for him to lean into his turn. He was going to give it just the right amount of throttle to send the bike scurrying around the corner and the silk scarf snapping out behind him. As he leaned into the turn the wind changed and the scarf wrapped around his face completely blinding him. The bike started to wobble and he reached for the pavement with his foot while trying to stop and balance the bike all at the same time. From somewhere close to his helmet he heard a deep voice from the crowd saying, "Use the Force, Luke, use the Force!"

As you can see it just never ends. So once again it's time to let our men and women in blue, and the ones in brown too, share with you their funniest moments, their embarrassing foibles, and their most hilarious memories as I embark on yet another journey into Tales From The Police Locker Room Volume II.

CHAPTER ONE

My Grandmother, rest her soul, always told me, "Son, it's a poor pair 'o legs that'll see the body hurt." I listened well to her advice. I spent most of my young life walking away from fights and then joined the police service. I'm sure if she were alive today she'd have a few choice words for me now too! I still don't really care to scrap all that much but it sort of comes with the territory.

I recall assisting another constable with an arrest one night. We had to take a guy down on a traffic warrant and he decided he was not going to leave his house. We informed him that he had no choice in the matter and would of course have to accompany us in our lovely police car. He made some uncouth remark about fornicating in other locations and grabbed my partner. His intent was definitely not to do-si-do although we did 'waltz' quite a bit trying to take him into custody. By the time we got him to the police car my tie was gone, my shirt

14

was ripped, he had lost one shoe, his belt buckle had come undone, his pants were around his knees and his face was buried in my armpit as I held him in a very tight headlock. We entered the rear seat of the car rather unceremoniously and began the trek to the police station. He stopped struggling but I was not going to release my grip on him. After a few moments I heard a muffled voice under my arm, "Why do I do this to myself?"

What's in a name? Well, in some cases there is the possibility of a partnership which may go down in history just because of the combination. Here are a few partnerships I have been made aware of over the years which still leave a certain feeling ringing in the air when you voice them:

Constable Hand and Constable Manyfingers, Constable Rose and Constable Lillies, Constable Dicken and Constable Dickhout, Detective John Smith and Detective Robyn Hood, Constable Police and Constable Constable, Constable Christmas and Constable Easter, Constable Boxer and Constable Dukes, Detective Johns and Detective Hooker, Constable Heavens and Constable Doors, Constable Hi and Constable Lo, Constables Hi and Jacks (of the Airport Detail), Constable Harley and Constable Davidson, Constable Luke and Constable Warm, Detective Plante and Detective Crooks, Constable Long and

Constable Shoren, Constable Clippet and Constable Barber.

Hey, I just writes 'em the way I gets 'em! On that note time for me to get back into some of the stories I have been collecting again. So sit back, strap your sides in so you don't burst all over, and read with me more of those wonderful Tales From The Police Locker Room Volume II.

*   *   *

Police officers love to play practical jokes on each other, especially when they know the reaction they'll get from the joke. We had a female constable in our area on whom we loved to play jokes. One day while she was out of the office a couple of the guys and I took four Henderson Directories and placed them under the legs of her desk. For those of you who don't know the directory it's about six inches thick. We moved a couple of the waste baskets alongside her desk to hide the legs. Her desk was butted up to mine, so we spread papers, files and junk where the two desks met to hide the difference in height.

She arrived shortly from court, flustered as hell from having lost a case, and proceeded to flop down and start on some of her paperwork. This constable sounded very much like Edith Bunker when she spoke and even more so when she was upset. Her voice went up about three notches in tone and she developed almost a southern drawl.

She had been working for a few minutes when she stopped, looked at her desk and asked, "What's wrong with my chay-er?"

Up she stood and fiddled with the positions for a moment and then plunked herself back at the desk. She began to unload about the case she had been on in court and was relating some inane decision rendered by the judge when she stopped mid-sentence, stood up again and asked, "What's wrong with my chay-er?"

Thinking someone must have switched it she changed with another chair and sat down again. We, of course, were all intent on her story and keeping our faces as straight as possible. It was hard to do - watching her struggle with paperwork with the desk blotter directly underneath her chin. All the while we also had been pressing the levers on our chairs and we had sunk ours down almost to her level.

"There's something wrong with my chay-er!" she said emphatically and stood up again.

"No," I replied almost resting my chin

17

on my desk top, "there's nothing wrong with your chair. There's nothing wrong with our chairs either."

Not wanting to accept our statements she grabbed her chair and went into the hall. We watched for the next thirty minutes or so while she swapped her chair with every one on our floor. After switching every one of them she ended up with her own chair back and still had not noticed the directories under her desk legs.

It took her three days to discover what we had done. Our only regret was that we didn't have it on video. I'm sure we would have been ten thousand dollars richer on America's Funniest Home Videos.

*   *   *

We had just come from the scene of a very serious injury hit and run. Our job was to gather exhibits at the scene - things like car parts, clothing pieces and such, and to take them to the hit and run office where we would identify each piece, tag it and log it for evidence. The exhibit room was relatively small and we had to work in very close quarters together to finish the task before the end of shift.

My partner was bent over the table cataloguing some very small pieces of debris and I was about to bag some clothing which had blood on it. I retrieved a pair of rubber gloves for the job and snapped them on with a resounding 'slap, slap'. I stood behind my partner and placed a hand on his shoulder while I reached over to retrieve a piece of clothing. I was pressed up against him in this manner when our inspector walked past the open door.

He stopped, cocked his head to one side, raised his eyebrows and asked, "Been partners too long, boys?"

* * *

While working night shifts a few of us would regularly patronize a local restaurant. It was comfortable, out of the way, and we had a good rapport with the staff. I had worked with the same partner for a long time and I should have know better, but I guess some of us never learn. Every damned time we went to pay the bill he would take one of those round toothpicks from the holder and stick me in the ass with it. Of course I would let out a yelp and the other patrons in the restaurant would look our way. By then my partner had either left or was standing there with this angelic look on his face shrugging his shoulders.

We got to be kinda like Lucy, Charlie

Brown and the football. "No, I won't do it again, okay, stab, yelp, wrong, I lied." This went on for quite a while.

One night I decided enough was enough. This time I let my partner go first and when we got to the cash register I retrieved a toothpick and promptly jabbed him with fervour in the ass. I struck him square in the wallet, broke the toothpick off and drove it into the palm of my hand. Of course I yelped again, he turned to the patrons, shrugged his shoulders and left with that damned angelic look on his face.

*   *   *

I was in court on a criminal matter and was waiting for the case to be called. You never know what's going to happen and some of the strangest things do.

When the first case was called the accused got up and went to the prisoner's box. The judge looked around the courtroom for a lawyer and then asked the young man, "You should have counsel. This is a more serious matter than you realize."

The man stood up in the box and replied, "I have the best counsel I can get."

Again the judge looked around the courtroom, and not seeing any lawyers he inquired, "And whom may I ask is that?"

"Jesus Christ in Heaven," the man stated.

The judge looked at the man over his glasses and replied, "I was thinking maybe of someone locally."

* * *

There is an older apartment building in the downtown area that has many low income tenants. Most of them are nice folk but there are a few drinkers we get regular calls from. One night we were sent to a disturbance at one of the units and when we got there I knocked on the door. We could hear some arguing going on inside but it didn't sound all that serious.

I knocked again and we heard a woman, obviously intoxicated, reply, "Eeyah, hoosz a my door?"

I asked, "Are you having a problem ma'am?"

"Yebetcha," she said, "I gotta guy 'n here an' I wan him out, out, outta my playsh!"

I winked at my partner and leaned closer to the door. "Do you want me to call the police ma'am?" I asked.

"Eeyah," she mumbled, "an' get thish sumbitch out, out, outta here!"

"Watch this, " I said to my partner with

a smile. I waited for a count of three and then knocked on the door with great authority.

The lady inside answered, "Hoosz there?"

"City Police," I said.

There was a brief pause and then she said, "Holy shit yoose guys are fast!"

*   *   *

K-9 was a great place to work and I had a great dog to work with. We went through some close calls together and really became quite close. His name was Lord and he earned it. He was a beautiful German Shepherd.

One day I was out taking Lord for a walk while off duty. I was in the alley behind my house and ran across a neighbour so we stopped to talk. After a brief conversation I turned to look for my dog but he was gone. I looked up and down the alley but he was nowhere in sight.

I yelled at the top of my lungs, "Lord!"

No answer - no dog.

I yelled again, "Lord, come!"

Still no answer - no dog.

"Lord, come!" I was getting rather frustrated.

Just then a lady who was in her garden, and had been down behind the fence while I was calling, stood up and looked at me.

"Sonny," she said, "it's just not time yet."

* * *

The Police Service Pipe Band is a proud unit. I was thrilled when I applied to join as a novice tenor drummer and was accepted. The thought of eventually getting my uniform and being able to march and perform as a member enthralled me. I used to practice all the time. The tenor drummer is the guy who has his drum sticks on loops and he twirls them around in all sorts of fancy manoeuvres. I worked my fingers raw every day in hopes of shortening the time I would have to wait before becoming a full member.

I took my dog for a walk one day in the lane and was busy practicing my twirling. I was getting pretty good - I could twist and turn and flip and flap without much ado. However, I hadn't gone two blocks when I was confronted by a patrol car.

"Freeze," the officer said, getting out of the car and pointing at me.

I recognized him and stepped forward dropping the sticks to my side.

"What's goin' on?" I asked, slipping the sticks from my hands in case he needed assistance in arresting some heinous criminal.

"It's you," he said with a giggle.

"Yeah, it's me," I said, "what about me?"

"Two of your neighbours called in when they saw this idiot walking down the back alley practicing with Nan-chukas! They figured he might kill somebody or hurt himself."

I practice my tenor swings at home now.

*   *   *

I'm one of the black cops in our department. I went to arrest a guy on a warrant and when he answered the door I noticed he was Latino and not much different in skin colour than me.

"Get your coat on, I got a warrant for you," I said to him, taking a jacket from the rack and passing it to him.

The guy took the coat, flung it around his shoulders vehemently, and glared at me.

After putting on his shoes he stood up and looked into my eyes.

"The only reason you're bustin' me is 'cause I'm not white," he spat at me.

I wrinkled my forehead, pinched my cheek and pointed at my face. "Try that one on the judge if you think he'll buy it," I said, placing the handcuffs on him and grinning.

*   *   *

A long long time ago we used to go into the farmland area outside the city limits on night shift. We would set up a few targets and take some practice shots because we didn't have a pistol range on the police department back then. We knew how long we could stay there before the farmer would call the Mounties to complain about kids shooting on his land. We always managed to get out of there before they got there.

One night we were a little too engrossed in our practice and didn't notice the Mountie's headlights coming across the field until it was too late. "Get into the cruiser," my partner hollered at me and we dove together.

He started the engine and hit the overhead light. Off we flew bouncing across the field like an old buck board.

"Shoot out the window," he hollered at me.

"At what?" I yelled back.

"Just shoot, I'll do the talking," he cried as the car careened towards an embankment.

I looked over my shoulder and as my head struck the roof of the car on a huge jolt

I saw the Mountie car with its overheads on pulling in behind us. I stuck my gun out the window and fired a round or two at the ground and as I did my partner reached the edge of the embankment. He thought he could travel down the slope but the car high-centered and we became hopelessly stuck.

"Jump out, run down the hill, and shoot again," he yelled as he bolted from the car and drew his weapon.

I blindly followed suit and the two of us ran down the grassy embankment firing rounds. When we got to the bottom we stopped and I looked at him thinking he was really daft. Out of breath we climbed back up to our car and the waiting Mountie.

"Did you see it?" my partner asked the Mountie who was regarding both of us with his eyebrows raised.

"Did I see what?" he asked, rolling his eyes.

"That rabbit with rabies. We've been tracking him for hours . . . almost had him that time."

"Right," said the Mountie.

"He was terrifying some children at the city limits," my partner continued.

"Right," said the Mountie.

"We seem to be stuck. Can you call a tow truck for us?"

"Right," said the Mountie, turning and

getting back into his car.

We never went back out there for target practice.

*   *   *

I don't know how it ever got started, but we went through a period where we used to steal each other's police cars. We would wait until the car crew was at a call and then we would sneak up and move their car. It was never far away but it was a hoot to watch them try to find it.

One car crew got a little out of hand and started playing jokes a little more serious than just taking the car. When you found it you never knew what was going to be in it - a bag of garbage, a cat, a chicken - it could be anything.

We decided to get them back. One night they parked their car at a usual coffee spot and went inside. We were hiding in the bushes and after a while I snuck over and used a spare set of keys to move the car. We took it across the parking lot and I got out. My partner had a jar of Vaseline and he spread a very thin coat over the front seat. We then opened two large bags of confetti and sprinkled

28

them over the Vaseline.

While he was finishing that I let the air out of the two rear tires and then placed a newspaper on the seat so I could move the car again. I drove it directly into the middle of a large puddle and parked it. My partner helped me out with a plank and we waited in the bushes.

Soon the car crew came out of the restaurant and started looking for their car. We could hear them mumbling and swearing under their breath. "How the hell are we going to explain this? Our damn car got stolen."

Finally they took out their flashlights and found the car in the puddle. One of the guys took off his shoes and socks and waded out to the door. We were in fits! These guys really deserved this. He got in, slammed the door, and started the car. We could hear him put it into gear and try to drive away. Ziiiizzzz, ziiizzzz . . . the wheels were spinning in the mud in the bottom of the puddle.

Out they got and groped around to find they had a flat tire. They cursed again, took out the jack, and changed the tire. By now they were both soaked from asshole to breakfast time and I'd say they were a little perturbed. They started the car again and guess what? Zziiiizzz, zziiiizzz. By the time they found the second flat tire they were fuming. They had to roll it down to the nearest service station and get some air in it. It was then they noticed these little paper confetti things stuck all over the backs of their uniforms. Brush as they might the stuff wouldn't come off because of the Vaseline.

When they got the tire back on and went back to the station they tried to blow the car out with an air hose and of course the Vaseline-covered confetti just stuck to everything it touched. They were there for hours blowing this stuff from the front seat to the back seat and back again.

At the end of shift they were still driving around covered in this stuff and we pulled our car alongside theirs at the office. As they were getting out with these wonderful little coloured dots all over them I said, "So, you like to steal police cars do you?"

That was the last time we ever had a problem with them.

*　　　*　　　*

I was with the RCAF during World War II and we flew into Winnipeg one day. We jumped into a car and decided to drive to Portage in our flying suits. There were four of us: pilot, co-pilot, a USAF pilot on training, and an air crewman. We stopped at the local tavern and quaffed a few before heading back to our plane where we were going to bed down for the night.

As luck would have it we were stopped by an RCMP officer who I swear was on his first hour out of Regina Training Depot. I mean this guy was so young we wanted to ask him if his mother knew he was out so late, and he was so polished that we could see our faces in his leathers. He was busily writing out the ticket when the pilot in the back seat got an idea.

He leaned forward and stuck his head out of the window.

"Constable," he barked, "aren't you supposed to stand at attention when you're in the presence of a Queen's Officer?"

The Mountie looked at him and suddenly recognized his uniform.

"Yes, sir," he said, bolting to attention, "You're right, sir."

He stood at attention for a moment and then began writing the ticket again.

The pilot leaned forward and yelled at him, "Stand at attention until I tell you different!"

The poor guy dropped his summons folder and stood straight as an arrow . . . as we drove off into the night. I hope he didn't stay there too long.

*   *   *

We were set up on a booze shack when the observer saw a car leave the house with a case of bootlegged beer. He radioed us to take the guy down and we raced off after him. We got him stopped and I made the arrest, seizing a case of beer from the car, and getting the drunk out of his vehicle. I'm a rather lightweight police woman and my partner was getting a chuckle out of watching me hold the guy up and try to stuff him into the rear seat of the police car. I got him inside and my partner, without thinking, tossed the case of beer onto the floor of the our car right beside the bad guy. This was a minor offence and I hadn't bothered to cuff the guy, so we headed off to the office to lay the appropriate charges. We drove a few blocks and all of a sudden I heard a clinking of glass. In a flash the guy pulled a bottle of beer from the case, twisted off the cap, and started chuggalugging the contents. I reached back to grab his wrist and at the same time my partner jammed on the brakes. The bad guy came flying forward, I twisted the bottle out of his hand, and dumped the beer onto his lap. Of course he started to fight and I had to hold him down until the car got stopped. In the melée I heard this funny sounding pop and the front hook of my bra snapped. I was still struggling with him when

I noticed my partner sitting there with this funny grin on his face watching me wobble all over the place.

When we got the bad guy to the office and put him in an interview room he started to complain about having beer spilled on him. I looked him in the eye and said, "You spilled beer all over my clean uniform, scraped my elbow on the dashboard, and busted my bra . . . and you're complaining!"

He didn't have a comeback.

*   *   *

I spent my early policing years with Scotland Yard in England. I came to Canada a few years back and became a policeman in this country where very different things happen than at home.

I was working as a district sergeant when I received a call stating that a bear had shown up in a city park on the outskirts of town and was terrorizing the citizens. I arrived on the scene and sure enough there was a bear off in the distance near the river. I called for Fish and Wildlife and when they got there, the warden took out his shotgun and came to the window of my van, in which I might add, I had remained.

"Well," he said, "you're in charge, what

do you want me to do?"

"You're Fish and Wildlife aren't you?" I asked.

"Yeah," he replied, raising one eyebrow.

"Well," I continued, "bears have been extinct in my country for five hundred years. I guess you're in charge."

*   *   *

We used to go to the city cells and get volunteer prisoners to stand in lineups when we were conducting one. They didn't mind doing it because it got them out of the cells for a few hours and gave them something to do.

We chose our seven guys and they each got to pick there own number for a position on the line. One of the inmates went through the numbers about six times before he finally chose one and then went up into the staging area to get ready. The lights went on and the instructions were given. They all made the required turns and finally the victim picked number four, which we were thankful for because he was our real bad guy.

As the other inmates were filing out and tossing their numbers back into the box, one of them turned to me and said, "This is my lucky day!"

"Why's that?" I asked him.

"I went through those numbers six times and I almost took number four. I could have been in real trouble."

* * *

I like to have fun when I'm working. I figure, what the heck, if you can't enjoy yourself and have a few laughs, why be here? I was working Checkstop one night when I saw a car coming towards me with a case of beer on the roof. Well, I jusr had to talk to these gfuys, so I pulled them over.

"Evening, boys," I said with a smile.

"Evening Officer," they replied.

"Anything to drink tonight?"

"Oh no, sir" the driver said, "we're all under age. We don't drink."

"Are you absolutely sure?" I asked them all over.

"Absolutely, Officer," came the reply form the back seat.

"Fine," I said "have a nice night and drive carefully.

"Thank you," they chorused together, and I could see the grins as they thought they had outsmarted me.

Just as the car pulled away I reached ovr and plucked the unopened case of beer from the roof.

Moments later I pulled a second car into the Checkstop. I had this case of beer behind my back.

"Evening," I said to the driver.

"Hello," he said politely.

"Anything to drink tonight?" I asked.

"Not yet," he replied, "but it's my birthday and I'll be having a few later."

"Well, happy birthday," I said, passing the case of beer in through his car window.

He was so dumbfounded he didn't know what to say. He just drove slowly away shaking his head.

*   *   *

There I was in my dirtiest, grubbiest undercover clothes consisting of a bag lady outfit. I was on a stakeout and expecting to make a move on the bad guy anytime when a police car pulled up beside me. They jumped out, tussled me to the ground, threw the handcuffs on me and tossed me into the back of their car. In a split second we were gone.

"You idiots!" I yelled. "I'm a police woman for Chrissake and I'm on a stakeout!"

"We know who you are," one of them said to me. "We got an urgent message that you are needed in court as a witness and that was the only way we could get you out of there without blowing your cover."

"Oh," I said, twisting the cuffs around so he could take them off.

They dropped me off at the courthouse and I went in to give my evidence. Being called as a surprise witness I had to explain my appearance to the judge and he accepted it. When I was done giving testimony and was about to step from the witness box, the prosecutor spoke up.

"Excuse me, Your Honour," he said, "but I have been informed that there are friends of the accused in the courtroom today who have threatened the life of this witness and I do not believe it is safe for her to leave in the normal manner. Might I ask that she be escorted out the back way?"

"Of course," replied the judge, and instructed the security officer to escort me out the rear exit.

He opened the door for me and I knew he just appreciated my greasy unwashed hair and my dishevelled appearance because as I stepped past him he closed the door behind me. I thought the guy was going to walk me out, but here I was all by myself in a huge hall with about six identical doors. I had no idea which one lead to the exit so I decided to try my luck.

I grabbed the handle and pushed on the heavy oak. It swung open with ease and

I stepped through. I was startled to find myself behind the empty judge's chair in the next courtroom. Of course the room was full and the clerk stood to her feet without looking at me.

"All rise," she said in her monotone, and the entire courtroom rose to their feet. The bad guy was already in the prisoner's box. He took one look at me and said with a grin, "All right, Your Honour, I'm a cinch to win this one!"

With that the court clerk turned to look at me and her mouth dropped open. I thought she was going to faint.

"Damn," I said, "forgot my robe again. Everybody chill, I'll be right back." I could hear the gasp as I walked out the door chuckling to myself.

Chapter Two

Hi again. So you liked book one so much you just had to run out and buy book two. Well I'm glad you did and you will be too. The nice thing about this book is that I haved been told stories by those who read book one and said, "Oh. I have a better story than that." They looked me up and I took them at their word - so to speak.

Speaking of picking up a book, I got a call from a police department which will remain annonymous, who wanted to inform me that they had just picked up a person shoplifting TALES FROM THE POLICE LOCKER ROOM from a store, Now, come on, not only is it bad business to get caught shoplifting, but to get caughht with a stolen police book in your booty!

Here's another kick at Murphy. You remember him from the last book? I'll tell you a bit more about him later , but I wanted to get my licks in early, so here I go

MORE OF MURPHY'S POLICE LAW.

1)   Never share a police car with any-

one braver than you are.

2) No search warrant take-down plan survives contact with the bad guys.

3) Friendly fire ... ain't.

4) The most dangerous thing at a major incident is a supervisor.

5) The problem with the great cover you have just found at a gun fight is that the has given you the wrong address and your are standing in the bad guy's line of fire.

6) The partner system is essntial to a police officier's survival: it gives the bad guy someone else to shoot at.

7) The closer you are to the hub of the action at a shooting incident the more likely you are to get shot in the ass by a cop.

8) Quartermaster Supply has only two sizes: too large and too small.

9) If you really need to see a supervisor in a hurry do something against policy.

10) Don't be conspicuous; in a shooting incident it draws fire, onroutine duty it draws supervisors.

After that bit of wisdom it's time I let the guys n' gals in blue tell a few more of their stories.

*   *   *

I was on the beat when my partner called me from a few blocks away to assist him in investigating a possible break and enter. I ran to the scene and he showed me a pile of what appeared to be band equipment lying just inside the door of a church. As we stepped inside I said to him, "I'll check the main hall, you go downstairs." He agreed and disappeared into the darkness of the hall. I took out my flashlight, and as I turned it on, I remembered I had not put in the fresh batteries I was supposed to at the beginning of shift.

In the dim orange light I tried my best to see where I was going and not to make too much noise which might spook the bad guys. I strode down the aisle, my breath coming in slow steady whispers, and my heart beginning to louden with the adrenalin pumping into me. As I stepped ever so carefully I realized I was walking on newspaper - sheet after sheet of newspaper. I lifted the beam of my light and shone it on the pulpit area. There I could see in the orange glow a stage and some panels from what appeared to be some type of church play.

I couldn't make out the writing and the designs on the wall so I slipped up the stairs onto the pulpit area. My light was really getting dim and I banged it three or four times to get more life out of the dying batteries. As I was banging the light I stepped forward and caught my toe on something. I lunged towards centre stage and found myself on a set of stairs. Trying desperately to maintain my balance I lurched down the steps and ran headlong into the waist deep water of the baptismal font. Just then my partner turned on the sanctuary lights and there I was, thrashing around like John the Baptist.

*   *   *

Guns are dangerous. Even if it's your issue gun it's still bloody dangerous. I was at the back counter one night with a particularly belligerent arrest. He was struggling and I was trying to hold him and the sergeant was telling me that we had a new rule. We had to leave our guns in a locker at the back counter before putting our prisoners in the cell. It was for safety reasons, he told me. Right.

As I continued to scuffle with the bad guy I decided it would be easier to take my gun and pass it to the sergeant who could lock it up. Just as I reached for it the bad guy turned and tried to twist out of my grip. He pulled me off balance and I grabbed the first solid thing I could find to hang on to - my gun handle. Training kicked in and my finger went directly to the trigger. Kah-blooey!!! I blew the bottom out of my new holster, destroyed a perfectly good pair of uniform pants, and put a nasty hole in the cement floor. The ricochet must have bounced off everything in the area before narrowly missing the sergeant. Everybody hit the floor and there was the guilty party left standing there with his face hanging out and turning a bit red.

As the smoke and debris cleared my partner peaked over the counter at me and said, "Okay, who wants to start the statements?"

*   *   *

I, like many other men before me, have had a vasectomy. It's a rather private thing that I don't talk about too much and I wanted it to stay that way. I also have a part-time business in which I deal a lot with the public. That I don't keep private.

One night my partner and I went to our favourite Chinese restaurant for our dinner break. We knew the owner very well and in fact I had quoted a job for him through my company. His English was not the best but he was very friendly and always made a point of coming to our table to speak with us. This night the place was packed and we were trying not to be too noticeable.

The owner walked up to our table and in a loud voice asked me, "How you penis?"

I turned a thousand shades of red and said with alarm, "What?"

"You penis," he said again very loudly, "how you penis?"

By now every eye in the restaurant was on me and I was ready to crawl under the table. How the hell did this guy find out about my bloody vasectomy? I must have looked completely bewildered because he leaned over my table and said, "You know, you give me quote on job, I want to know how you company doing."

*   *   *

An impaired driver failed to negotiate a turn and bounced unceremoniously down an embankment onto a railroad track. "When we arrived at the scene we could see the car straddling and facing up the tracks." I walked up to the car and noted that the engine was still running and the driver was holding the steering wheel staring straight ahead. I tapped on the window with my flashlight and the guy looked over at me with a sleepy grin.

"Yes, officer," he said with a heavy slur,

"and what may I ask are you pulling me over for?"

*   *   *

A few years ago we had a gun amnesty. That's where we tell everyone who has guns that are not registered they can bring them into the office and we will send them away for destruction. It's supposed to be a simple job but it's the only time the front counter personnel wear bullet proof vests. A lot of the people bringing them in are not trained in handling procedures and we spend a lot of time ducking behind the counter. We also accept ammunition which has been outdated or is left over from when the owner had a weapon of some type.

A person arrived at our location with two cans of black powder. Most of the guys on our shift had never seen black powder and I decided to tell them how dangerous it was in a can. As they pressed me I agreed to take the powder into the back parking lot, pour it on the ground, and light it to demonstrate the power of the powder.

"Isn't that dangerous, Inspector?" one of the guys asked.

"Only if you don't know what you're doing," I replied.

We all went to the parking lot and gathered around as I poured the powder into a

pile. I struck a match and dropped it. Nothing! I struck another match. Nothing! Three more matches. Nothing!!!

"Looks like it isn't going to light," I said to the group.

"Naw, you just need more power, oo,oo,oo," said a sergeant, stepping from the crowd with his notebook in hand. He tore a few pages out, made them into a tube, and lit it.

I had moved away and lost interest because I was convinced it wasn't going to light. Out of the corner of my eye I saw a single spark fall from the paper onto the top of the pile of powder. What followed was the biggest explosion one man ever told another about! As I turned I thought I was looking into the sun. The blast hit me and blew my coat half off. I could feel my hair melting. I saw the sergeant staggering across the parking lot with his hair on fire and there were pieces of uniform gently floating down in the evening breeze.

One of the guys, whose face was black from the explosion, came over to me and made the understatement of the year, "Inspector, I think you're burned."

"No shit!" I said, putting my hand to my face. "Where the hell are my eyebrows?"

"I'd say they're coming down in the next province about now," someone said from the crowd.

As a direct result of this incident the following piece of poetic solace arrived on my desk very quickly:

* * *

T'was just weeks before Christmas
In Police District Three;
Black Powder they had
Because of gun amnesty.
"What do we do?"
Asked the Sergeant with glee.
The Inspector replied,
"Follow me and you'll see."
To the back lot they went
All anxious to see
The Inspector's great show,
Cause an EXPERT was he.
They all watched like children
As the powder was placed
Into a great pile,
And a fuse made in haste.
Matches were struck
Alas, to no avail.
So a notebook was lit,
Now that wouldn't fail!
The wind caught a spark
And the powder it blew,
Blowing up the Sergeant

And the Inspector too!
There they both stood,
Clothing in tatters,
Singed hair and egos,
Black Powder smatters.
The moral of the story
If it were told,
"Don't play with matches
'Round powder that's old!"

*   *   *

We suffered a lot of break-ins in a particular area of our beat and were not having much success in catching the bad guy. He was hitting business after business in the wee hours of the morning and we always seemed to be just a few steps behind him. We decided to stake out part of the area and were busy hiding in our patrol car when an employee of a local business drove up to us.

"Ya know," he said, "I could give yuh a lesson on howta ketch this guy if yuh were int'rested."

"What might that entail?" I responded, more out of amusement than interest.

"If I were yuh two young fellas, I'd grab me that big backhoe over yonder an' dig me a deep hole right about where yer settin'. Then, if I were yuh two, I'd cover it with a hunk o' thin plywood an' set back in the weeds a spell.

Never know whatcha might ketch."

"Well, thanks for the idea but I think we'll stick with real police work for now," I said.

"Welcum," he said, spitting a brown stream of chewing tobacco onto the ground beside the car and leaving.

Nothing happened for the entire shift except that our bad guy broke into a business two blocks away and we missed him again. This was getting to be a bad habit.

The following night we were given the word from our sergeant, "If you don't catch this guy tonight don't bother coming back to the office."

With our tails between our legs we drove quietly back to the same business we had staked out the night before. As we turned into the driveway we noticed that the second floor of the office building was lit up from the outside.

"I don't remember this place having floodlights," I said to my partner as we drove beside the wall.

Just as we reached the back corner of the building we saw a pair of vehicle headlights at a very strange angle and pointing to the sky. We approached cautiously and discovered a pickup truck buried to the centre, rear wheels down in a pit. The sides of the truck were bordered by two large pieces of very thin and broken plywood. The bad guy was trapped inside the truck and he was easy pickings for us. The truck was jammed full of stolen property and break and enter tools. Bingo! We had him.

Just as we were extricating him from the vehicle and placing him in handcuffs we heard a sound behind us. We turned to see someone in the shadows.

"Who's there?" I said into the dark.

"Nobody what counts," came the reply, "I'll jest let you two fellas get on with yer real p'lice werk".

He just disappeared like the Lone Ranger or one of those old cowboy heros, except he didn't leave a silver bullet, just some brown spit.

*   *   *

Sometimes you just should have stayed home. My partner had broken a shoelace, popped a button off an epaulette, dropped her clipboard into a mud puddle on the way to the car and was generally not having a good day.

We were on our way to make a meet with another car crew for coffee when we spotted a young guy walking and looking over his shoulder at us. We drove past him and made a quick u-turn to cut him off and see what his problem was. He jack-rabbited and we gave chase. He was fast and knew the area and we had trouble trying to get close to him with the car. Finally we managed to corner him on a construction site and my partner leapt from the passenger seat to tackle him.

I saw him run up a wall of dirt and knew there was a fence on the other side, so I decided to back up, drive around the dirt pile and cut him off again. I threw the transmission into reverse and stood on the gas pedal. Rocks and mud flew under the carbanging against the drive shaft and exhaust system with loud thumps and clangs. I was looking over my left shoulder so I wouldn't back into a post and it wasn't until I was ready to go forward that I realized something wasn't quite right. I turned to look at my partner's open door and there she was.

"Stop the damn car!" she was screaming at me with death threats in her eyes.

When I backed up with great force I had managed to snag her gun belt on the door latch. I then dragged her, rather unceremoniously, through thirty feet of mud and rocks with such force that her back pockets were full, as were her boots. Her flashlight was buried somewhere in the mud and you couldn't see the butt of her gun for mud and rocks.

She unhooked herself from the door,

glared at me, and then ran with such energy that she caught the bad guy about a block away. She didn't speak to me for two days. Probably better that she didn't because I couldn't have said 'I'm sorry' with a straight face.

*   *   *

Rookies make good material. Sometimes we think of them as raw meat and we do some really nasty things to them. It's all in fun and part of the initiation and they take it so well. That's how they learn to dish it out when they become senior. We do things to them like telling them if you arrest a bad guy on a "bench warrant" you have to sit on the bench beside your prisoner when the judge comes in for the bail hearing; or convincing them that a particularly terse superintendent with no sense of ha-ha prefers to be called 'Supe', or that the siren doesn't work and he'll have to stick his head out the window and yell at the motorists to get out of the way.

A very seasoned member was training out a very young rookie. This in itself is a recipe for a little fun. The veteran officer was talking on the radio and had just hung up the mike when the rookie set himself up.

"What makes that little sound every time you stop talking into the mike?" he asked.

"What sound is that?" asked the trainer, grinning inside.

"It sounds like static every time you stop talking," said the rookie, picking up the mike for the first time and handling it like an alien artifact.

The sound actually is static which is caused when you release the mike transmit button.

"Oh that," said the trainer, "didn't they tell you about that in police college?"

"No," said the rookie, leaning forward to gain a gem of knowledge from his older and wiser partner.

"Every time you finish speaking into the mike you have to make that sound in the back of your throat. It's sorta like the sound a cat makes when it's got a hairball stuck, you know, like 'h-h-h-h-h-I-I-I-I-c-c-c-h-h-h-h'. It's called radio etiquette to let the other person know you are finished your transmission. Try it."

"H-h-h-h-u-u-u-u-c-c-c-c-k," said the rookie.

"Not quite," said the trainer, "more in the back of your throat and into your nose."

"H-h-h-h-I-I-I-I-c-c-c-h-h-h," said the rookie with a grin.

"You got it!" yelped his trainer, patting him on the shoulder, "and faster than I ever trained anyone before. Now go ahead, try it out."

The rookie took the mike gingerly in his hands and lifted it to his mouth. He keyed the mike and looked at his trainer for reassurance. The trainer nodded.

"1254 to dispatch, h-h-h-h-I-I-I-I-c-c-c-c-h-h-h."

"Go ahead, 1254."

"Do you have any calls waiting in our area, h-h-h-h-h-I-I-I-I-c-c-c-c-h-h-h?"

"Nothing at all, thank you."

"1254, out h-h-h-h-I-I-I-I-c-c-c-c-h-h-h-h."

Time marched on and the rookie spent three weeks with the old trainer. He then was placed with a new trainer to receive a different perspective. They weren't five minutes on the street when they got their first call from dispatch.

"1117, respond," said dispatch.

The rookie grabbed the mike with fervour, "1117, go ahead h-h-h-h-I-I-I-I-c-c-c-h-h-h."

"I have a 10-11 for you; the address is on your CAD."

"10-4," said the rookie, grinning at his partner with confidence, "we're rolling, h-h-h-h-h-I-I-I-I-ic-c-c-c-h-h-h-h."

"What the hell is wrong with your throat?" asked the new trainer.

"Nothing. Why?" replied the rookie.

"What's that horrible noise you keep making? Sounds like you got a damn furball caught in your throat."

"That's what my last trainer told me to do after - each - radio . . ."

There was a long pause.

"I've been had haven't I?"

"Big time!" he said.

*   *   *

Here's the set up - I was working alcohol Checkstop, it was getting very late on in the shift, some of the drivers had been drunk, but I was getting 'punch drunk'. My partner and I were busy misbehaving and doing rap style dance steps between stopping vehicles. We were laughing hard but managed to get it under control when each driver pulled in.

It was my turn to check the car and I flagged over a very small import car. When I looked inside I couldn't believe my eyes; the guy driving weighed at least three hundred pounds. As I walked over to the car window to speak to him I noticed my partner with his hat and jacket on backwards doing a terrible version of Michael Jackson's moonwalk. I fought with every ounce of my strength not to burst into laughter as I approached the big guy in the car.

I was supposed to say, "Good evening, sir, alcohol Checkstop. Have you had anything to drink tonight?"

While being distracted by my partner and the size of the poorguy, I stuckmy head into the driver's window and said "Good evening, sir, alcohol Checkstop. Have you had anything to eat tonight?"

* * *

High adventure even manages to get itself in the way of the 'silly bug' and turns derring do into derring don't. Citizens often assist the police in catching bad guys but things don't always turn out like this. The Keystone Cops and Buster Keaton couldn't have done it better.

A call came in as a silent alarm at a gas station. We responded and were en route when a second call came in about some crazy with a rifle just south of our location. We broke away from the alarm and started towards the guy with the rifle call. Another car crew took our alarm call and were en route to it when the rifle call was updated to a shooting. The second car crew and a supervisor responded and now three of us were headed for the rifle call. A third car crew took our alarm call and were en route when the shooting was updated to a possible hostage taking. The new car crew joined us and the alarm went to hell. Now there were four cars descending on the scene and a K-9 car coming from the other end of the city to lend us a hand. Meanwhile, here's what was happening at the rifle call. A guy had been sleeping in his trailer in a parking lot nearby. He had awakened to the sound of breaking glass and looked outside to see a bad guy inside a service station, stuffing cigarettes into his pockets and running across the parking lot. (For you American readers, cigarettes in Canada are like gold. Our government has taxed them to about $6.00 a pack, so we're not crazy, some people really do steal cigarettes.) Mr. Citizen jumped out of bed and threw on his shoes. He grabbed his .22 rifle and leapt into action - wearing only his shoes and underwear. Oh, yes, the temperature was minus 38 degrees Celsius (for you American readers that's - damn cold!).

Another citizen saw the half naked guy

running around with the rifle and called it into police. The good guy caught up to the bad guy and ordered him to stop. The bad guy said, "Golly gee whilikers, mister, why don't you just leave me alone", or similar words. So the good guy raised his .22 and shot the bad guy in the back of the leg. Rather than slow the guy down it worked just the opposite and he got a jolt of adrenalin. He engaged his warp engines and left the half naked citizen standing alone.

Mr. Citizen spotted a taxi and raced over to him waving the .22 in the air. Now picture this from the point of view of the taxi driver. You have just witnessed a half-naked crazy man in shoes and underwear at minus 38 degrees shoot someone in the leg. Now the idiot is running towards you yelling at you to stop. Right! You're gonna stop and check it out!

Just as the taxi driver called the confusion into his dispatcher the guy with the rifle reached his car and started banging on the window. He was yelling, "Get that guy! Follow him!"

The taxi driver was trying to drive away when the guy jumped onto the hood of his car and grabbed the wiper blades. He started banging on the window and screaming, "Follow him, follow him!" Deciding that discretion was the better part of valour the taxi driver called his dispatch again, updating the situation, and followed the bad guy.

By now half the police cars in the city were on their way. The radio was so full of chatter that the responding cars could neither hear dispatch nor pass any information on - as has a habit of happening during 'glory calls'. Police cars were passing each other, cutting each other off, taking alleys and driving the wrong way on one-way streets. It was chaos!

Meanwhile, back at the rifle call, the taxi with the half-naked hood ornament had caught up to the bad guy who was now running out of steam and was throwing packages of cigarettes out of his coat like a crew member distributing life jackets on the Titanic. When the taxi got close enough the rifle guy jumped from the hood and tackled the bad guy. They were rolling around in the ice and snow when the first police cars arrived on the scene.

By now the taxi driver was outside his car and waving frantically. The first car on the scene jumped into the fight and grabbed a body. It was only seconds before many more cars arrived and every policeman there wanted in on the action. Two guys grabbed the taxi driver while two more latched onto the rifleman. In a moment the chaos began to subside.

One officer asked the taxi driver, "What's your name?"

"Lovette," he said.

"I know," said the cop, "I do too, now what's your name?"

"Lovette," said the taxi driver.

"Listen," said the cop, "I don't have time for this. We can reminisce later. What's your name?"

"That's my name," said the cabbie, quite perturbed.

"Oh."

About that time someone else was asking the rifleman the same question.

"Shatz," he replied.

"Don't get smart with me, what's your name?" said the cop.

"Wilhelm Shatz is my damned name you idiot," the guy screamed back.

That wasn't the end of it. While all this was going on another cop was asking the thief what his name was.

"Leggo, you asshole," came the reply.

"I ain't lettin' go, now what's your gawddamn name?" yelled the cop.

"That's my name you stupid ass, Albert Leggo."

As I said, I don't think the Keystone Cops and Buster Keaton could have done it any better!

Your guess is as good as mine, but I think this one may have been embellished *just a tad!*

CHAPTER THREE

I just can't seem to stop! Only two chapters into the book and I've taken a few swings at just about everyone. Do youremember Murphy? I talked about him in the last chapter and in Book One TALES FROM THE POLICE LOCKER ROOM VOL. I (available at most bookstores ar..ar..ar..). He's the guy they named Murphy's Law after and we don't know any more about him. Ah yes, Murphy's Law, that wonderful thing no profession can escape. Just when you think you have all your plans in place the proverbial faeces hits the oscillator and your plans go for a dump. For example:

A certain apartment was known to be inhabited by persons who in the privacy of their humble abode would put illegal liquids into hypodermics and jam them into their arms. It was decided that these persons should be arrested so they could be removed to barred and locked facilities. There, other persons would rehabilitate them to the point where they could con the Parole Board and get out much earlier than expected, so they could go back to the apartment and put more illegal liquids into their arms.

In order to best take these mislead persons into custody the TAC Team was called in. These persons were known to have acquired certain illegal weapons, which had been stored by honest persons who were not permitted to use them, but would spend more time in jail than the bad guys if they did use them.

The decision was made to have one TAC Team member scale the outside of the building and make ready on the balcony. When he was given the command he was to do the following: break the window, jam his Mark 9 fire-extinguisher-sized canister of pepper spray through the hole, and commence to soak the inside of the apartment with the incapacitating vapour. Simultaneously the remainder of the TAC Team, awaiting the same signal in the hall, would ram down the door, jam a Mark 9 fire-extinguisher-sized canister of pepper spray through the open door, and commence to soak everything in the room like the guy on the balcony was doing.

The plan was set, the sergeant straightened his ball cap with one hand, drew his Glock semi-auto with the other and spoke the words of command into his mike. Like silken steel cats the men of valour leapt to the task, followed closely by Murphy! The tinkling sound of breaking glass on the balcony was nearly lost in the din of the metal ram shattering the apartment door into a thousand pieces. One TAC member fell to his knees and scanned the room with his weapon while the others pressed against the back of the man with the Mark 9. Singly, the two pepper sprayers let loose a volley of Oleoresin Capsicum which, in the report which followed, was only 'a two one-second burst', but managed to drench the inside of the room like Hurricane Andrew.

Murphy stuck his nose into the plan and this is where it began to disintegrate rather rapidly. As the two blasts of pepper spray coated the interior of the apartment, a cross draft was set up between the broken window and the door. As Murphy would have it a very heavy gust of wind came up, gathered all of the pepper spray into a huge cloud, and blew it directly into the faces of the entering TAC Team. They were all immediately incapacitated.

Oh, the bad guys? They were all in the bedroom sleeping off illegal liquids and didn'tget peppered at all.

Here are a few of Murphy's Rules. These go hand-in-hand with his Laws and obviously form an integral part in police officers making fools of themselves:

1) Bullet proof vests aren't.

2) The bigger they are, the harder they fall . . . also the harder they punch, kick and choke.

3) The speed at which you respond to a fight call is proportionate to how long you've been on the force.

4) High speed chases will always proceed from an area of light traffic to an area of extremely heavy traffic.

5) If you know someone who tortures animals and wets the bed, he is either a serial killer or works for Internal Affairs.

6) Placing a gun back into a shoulder holster with your finger on the trigger will cause you to walk with a limp.

7) If you have cleared all the rooms in a house and met no resistance, you and the entry team have probably kicked in the wrong house.

8) When you swing your baton in a fight you will hit more fellow officers than you will bad guys.

9) Domestic arguments always migrate from an area of few available weapons (living room) to an area with many available weapons (kitchen).

10) If you have just punched out a handcuffed prisoner for spitting in your face, you will undoubtedly be starring on the News Hawks at six o'clock.

11) If you drive your patrol car to the geometric centre of the Gobi Desert and stop, it will take less than five minutes for someone to pull alongside and ask, "Can I go through here?"

12) A poor shooter with a rifle is a better shot than an expert with a handgun.

13) From behind you, the bad guy can see your gun's night sights just as well as you can.

14) Never do a shotgun search of a dark warehouse with a partner whose nickname is "Boomer"!

It's time to see Murphy in real action again so I'll turn the story telling back to those

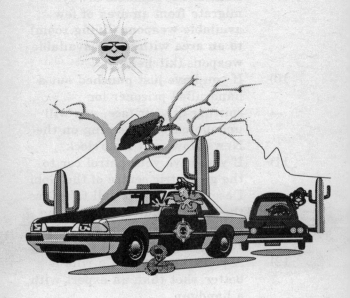

who do it best, the men and women who protect you (feel safe?), the solemn sisterhood and brotherhood of the Blue Line (no, no, not the Maple Leafs), your city's finest!!

*   *   *

"City Police, how can I help you?"

"I want my wife charged with buggery!"

"I beg your pardon!!"

"You heard me, I want a cop over here right now to charge my wife with buggery!"

"Maybe if you explain your problem to me, sir, I would be better able to direct your call."

"Sure. I came home drunk last night and my wife was yelling at me about snoring in my sleep when I drink. I told her I never snored, so she took a damned tape recorder and taped me snoring. Now I want her charged with buggery!"

"No sir, that's bugging, not buggery."

"Well then what the hell is buggery?"

"Uh . . . how can I best explain this? Buggery is . . . uh . . . when someone places a foreign object into the anus of another person."

"Then maybe you better send the cop over to charge me 'cause that's where I'm gonna jamb that tape recorder if she ever tapes me again!!!"

Dispatcher of Cops

*　　　*　　　*

I am happy to announce that now even the civilians are getting into the act and sending me stories. Here is one I just couldn't resist:

Free trade with the United States comes in many forms. We can buy and sell cars across the 49th parallel now, stereo equipment and computers and a variety of other items which are of interest to us. However, sometimes free trade involves those things we would never suspect.

Not too long ago I travelled to Reno, Nevada, for the weekend. I met a very talkative group of Canadians and Americans while at one of the card tables. During our conversation it was mentioned that speed limits on the Nevada Interstate highways were meaningless. A person travelling about ten miles per hour over the posted speed limit seemed to be the norm. Nonof the players at our table could recall seeing a motorist stopped for speeding by a Nevada police officer.

The dealer at our table grinned widely as she deftly turned a card in front of me. I was sure she had a straight flush hidden. But instead she set us all straight and without a flush.

"In order to be stopped by the Nevada State Patrol," she said, "you must first have some very specific qualifications."

"And what might those be?" I asked, looking at my last card and realizing I was not going to make the flush I had hoped for, not the one on the table anyway. Maybe the one in the bathroom.

"Now listen closely boys," she said, flipping her cards over to show a straight flush as I had suspected. "The first thing is that the vehicle must be a red Corvette. Once that qualification has been met we move onto number two. The driver must be a well-built, young, cute, blonde chick. If you meet those specifications you'll get yourself pulled over."

We all laughed, and mused over how it would be nice to be a cop for a while if we didn't have to stop the real bad guys, only the chicks.

Shortly after my return to Canada our province legalized slot machines and they began to appear everywhere. This was greatly influenced by our neighbours to the south and could be considered a free trade of ideas. I was leaving a casino one night when I noticed a city police officer running into the street and waving his hat. He was obviously stopping a car for speeding.

"Just how far does free trade go?" I asked myself with a chuckle and stood to watch.

What did he pull over - a cute, young, blonde lady in a red sports car. What can I say

free trade in action!

*   *   *

The dry English sense of humour. Nowhere in the world can it be topped for comedy even in real life. Here's yet another tale from the English courts that will . . . well, just read it.

A young constable was on foot patrol and on his beat he noted a motorist who was quite obviously speeding. Not having access to a radar with which to record the speed, nor to a police vehicle to pace the offender, the officer estimated the speed of the motorcar and subsequently had the driver charged with the offence.

At trial the motorist arrived with counsel and both were determined to have a field day with the constable. Their objective was to discredit him on the witness stand. How on earth could a pedestrian estimate a vehicle's speed well enough to secure a conviction?

The lawyer tried every angle possible to shake the young constable. Nothing was successful. The officer stood his ground and presented his evidence in a cool, calm, and professional manner. The lawyer became very frustrated and angry. In a final flurry of futility he picked up his pencil and threw it violently across the courtroom.

"Perhaps, Officer," he stated acidly, "you'd care to tell the court exactly how fast that pencil was travelling!"

The constable hesitated only briefly, then replied, "I can't say, Your Worship, the defendant was not driving a pencil."

*   *   *

One night a pellet gun was confiscated and brought back to the office of our small police department. It was a rather boring night and a few of the guys on shift decided to try the gun out to see if it really worked. Of course a target was required and they decided to use a calender which was hanging outside the chief's office.

Each took a few turns and were amazed at the accuracy of the little weapon. Numerous holes appeared in the face of the calender and one of the guys remarked how much force the pellet gun had. He took aim again and his need for practice was identified as the etched glass in the door to the chief's office exploded inward with a thunderous crash.

"How the hell will we explain this?" he asked, passing the gun to one of his fellow

officers.

"The chief will never accept any story we tell him and we're all done like dinner if we don't fix it."

Emergency calls went out and finally someone was located to attend the office and replace the broken window. While he was installing the glass, the constables went through the yellow pages frantically to find a glass etcher. He arrived and re-lettered the door. The officers were escorting him out the back door when the chief arrived via the front door. Saved in the nick of time, they were thinking to themselves.

"I even remembered to take down the calender full of holes," bragged one of them as they all entered the front door, innocent and smiling.

The chief was standing outside his office when they arrived. He looked at the four of them with their angelic grins, pointed to numerous holes in the wall where the calender used to be and said, "I want a full report on this now!"

Ever heard the expression 'Constable For Life'?

*   *   *

One of the members of our police commission is a Native Indian who wears very long braids. He is known to take the police department to task quite brilliantly and this day was no exception. The police commission had been embroiled in a disagreement with the department for weeks and the tension was very high on both sides.

When it came time for the Native member to question the chief he stood, held a portfolio in front of him eloquently, turned to the chief stone-faced and stood there.

After a brief silence the chief asked the member, "Is there some problem?"

The member grinned from ear to ear, dropped his portfolio onto the podium and replied, "I have trouble calling you chief. You don't have any braids."

*   *   *

Gravity is a funny thing. It causes all kinds of problems, but if we didn't have it we would all either float away or weigh three tons. Sir Isaac Newton discovered gravity when an apple fell on his head. All I can say is he's lucky he wasn't working in a blacksmith's shop that day.

I was standing on the sidewalk at 2:00 A.M. when I noticed that some person had left a beer bottle standing on the curb. I was going to pick it up when I saw that the street cleaner was approaching with its huge brushes and would probably pick it up easier than me.

I decided to tip the bottle over with my foot and let it fall into the gutter. When the machine came past the bottle would soon be gone. I leaned back and raised my foot to the height of the bottle neck. I kicked my leg forward, and to this day I don't know what happened. I got a twitch or something and I struck the bottle with full force. It lifted like a missile and flew in an incredible arc across the roadway. As I watched in horror, the tumbling, twisting bottle vaulted the entire street and struck the front window of a jewellery shop with sufficient force to blast the window into smithereens.

The alarm bell sounded and the shattering of glass could be heard for blocks. I was dumbfounded. Just then the street cleaner arrived. He stopped his machine and leaned out of the cab.

"That's the second time this month for that window," he yelled over the roar of the engine. "Good work you're here or some hooligans would run off with half the owner's stock."

"Yes," I replied, strolling to the corner to phone my station sergeant.

*   *   *

Magistrate's courts in England are often presided over by very old justices seemingly minutes away from retirement. The clerks of the courts are professionals, trained in the legal craft and generally run the court procedure for the justice.

On one occasion, a geriatric magistrate was hearing a case which centered around an incident which occurred outside a night club. The prosecution witness referred numerous times to the club as a 'discotheque'. The old magistrate was obviously becoming very confused. After hearing the term for the 'nth' time, he interrupted the proceedings with, "Discotheque? Discotheque? What is this Discotheque?"

The clerk turned to the old boy, and with a deadpan expression replied, "I believe, sir, it's one of those establishments where they play gramophone records."

The justice nodded and sat back.

*   *   *

I work a corner in our downtown area every day at the same time to write tickets for illegal turns. I have written so many over the years that I have become immune to most of the remarks made to me by motorists whom I ticket. This particular day was no different. I was churning out the tickets as fast as I could write them and the remarks were rolling off my back like bullets against my bullet proof vest.

The sun was shining and I was in a particularly good mood which caused me to whistle while I was working. I gave a man his ticket and turned away from his vehicle, whistling while I finished off my notes on the offence. The man jumped from his car, ran up to me, and grabbed my shoulder.

"I don't think that's very funny at all," he snapped at me.

"What?" I asked, not having any idea what he was referring to.

"That tune - the one you're whistling. That's not funny at all," he growled, returning to his car and driving away.

I shrugged my shoulders and went back to the corner to await my next offender. I began to whistle again and it was only then I realized I was whistling "Here's A Quarter, Tell Someone Who Cares."

*　　　*　　　*

Rookies have to band together. It's not only for survival on the street, it's for survival in the ranks as well. There were four of us and we had developed a pretty tight relationship in college. Our department was rather small and we maintained the camaraderie onto the street. It became painfully obvious that one in our ranks had become a terrible 'brown-noser' and he would stop at nothing to increase his own position. He stopped hanging around with us and refused to meet with us on shift for coffee. We decided it was time to teach him a lesson.

We were all working 2100 shift (9:00 P.M. civilian time) and were assigned to a warehouse district bordering on the CP Rail tracks. One of our guys talked to the rook and found out what time he was planning on being at a specific location. We jumped into our squad cars and roared off to the back of a supermarket. A brief rummage through the garbage bin turned up a number of overripe tomatoes and some pretty foul eggs. We loaded our pockets and went to work.

At the prearranged time we slid quietly into the area, and sure enough, there was our guy checking out warehouse doors. We parked our cars a distance away and retraced our route with catlike stealth. The three of us circled him, out of sight, and when the time was right we pelted him with tomatoes and eggs, being careful to stay low and out of sight.

Unknown to us, the rook had made arrangements to meet the CP Rail police, and in moments the area was flooded with them.

It took every bit of know-how and smarts to get back to our cars without getting caught.

"Home free!" I yelled as we jumped into our cars and took off.

I was just about to turn the headlamps on when I saw a CP police car turning the corner onto my street. In a deft move I spun the wheel and placed my car completely behind a loading dock. The CP police car slowed as he neared my location and turned on his search light. Just as the beam made a quick flash in my direction I threw myself onto the seat to be out of his sight. There came a terrible squishing and cracking sound as the remainder of the rotten tomatoes and eggs broke in my pockets. Within seconds I was nearly overcome by the fumes and I was gagging inside my car. The following day the incident was posted on the bulletin board at work and we were to assist the rook in locating his attackers. Needless to say they were never found, and I had to replace the uniform I had on that night.

* * *

English magistrate's courts are often split between morning criminal matters and afternoon traffic cases. A very experienced traffic patrol officer was giving evidence in a morning case. He had arrested a youth and charged him with using 'threatening, abusive or insulting words or behaviour'. This particular miscreant had used the word 'fuck' a number of times. The traffic officer provided the requisite evidence of the two passing nuns, who were obviously shocked at hearing such bad language, and things appeared to be leaning his way.

The magistrate recessed court for a few minutes, perhaps to look the word up in the dictionary. A short time later he returned with a landmark decision.

"The word 'fuck'," he stated, "has become so commonplace in our language that it can no longer possibly be construed as offensive or insulting! Case dismissed."

After lunch the court began hearing traffic matters and the same officer was giving evidence before the same magistrate. A motorist had been summonsed for operating a vehicle with a defective exhaust system. The officer was attempting to describe for the court the exact dimensions of the hole in the muffler when he was interrupted rather abruptly by the magistrate.

"Come, come, man we don't have all day," said the magistrate with distaste in his voice. "Be specific, use your hands and show me how big was the hole in the muffler!"

The officer turned to the magistrate, made a circle with his hands and replied, "This fucking big, Your Worship!"

*   *   *

I was working alone one evening and made a meet with a two-man car crew for coffee. We were just returning to our police cars when we witnessed a hit and run on a fence. We jumped into our cars and gave chase. When I had exited the restaurant I had purchased and opened one of those liquid yogurt drinks in my favourite flavour. I set the container on the dashboard and soon had the driver of the offending vehicle pulled over. When he stopped his vehicle he got out and ran. I chased him on foot and we tumbled into a yard during the fight.

The clatter we made could have awakened the dead; as a matter of fact it did. The guy who came out to see what was going on was dead drunk. He yelled at us and told me to leave the guy alone and began threatening to get involved in the fight. Just as he came down the steps towards our tumbling bodies the other car crew arrived and assisted me with the arrest. One of them managed to get the other drunk settled down, and we were ready to put the hit and run driver into my car when he started to fight again. We decided that I would take my drunken driver downtown with a partner and the odd man out would drive my car to headquarters for me. We poured the bad guy into the back seat of the police car and I tossed my car keys to the other constable. He strode to my car and waved as we passed him. Into the driver's seat he bounced, fired up the engine, dropped the transmission into drive and walked on the gas pedal. The car leapt forward - and the liquid yogurt leapt backward. The container bounced off the top of the steering wheel, turned upside down, and flew directly into his face. It hit him about the nose area and seemingly hung there until all of its contents were released. He was covered from asshole to breakfast time.

He arrived at headquarters moments after we did and stepped into the booking room.

"Aw man, you spilled my yogurt!" I teased.

"Don't even start!" was all he said as he headed for the showers.

*   *   *

Walking the beat in the old days wasn't so bad in the summer. It was the winter nights that made the cold run through your soul. I had worked the 2100 shift (Okay, this is a test civilians - what time is 2100? I told you once, were you paying attention?) and we were all back at headquarters to sign off. All but one of us that is. We waited about fifteen minutes and when our comrade still failed to show we became very concerned. What if he had been struck on the head by a bad guy and was lying out there somewhere, alone and freezing to death?

The duty sergeant made the decision and we were all sent out along with day shift to find our missing brother. We combed his beat from one end to the other. Nothing! We began working our way back to the headquarters building, still checking every nook and cranny along the way. Finally someone noticed a service station bathroom door ajar and we all rushed to aid our potentially fallen comrade. We shoved the door open and crowded around the scene determined to handle whatever we found inside. Oh, he was there all right, on the toilet, pants around his ankles, wrapped tightly in his buffalo coat . . . sound asleep!

CHAPTER FOUR

The "Greying of the Blue" is a new buzz term which has been heard in many politico-statistical police circles. It's commonly used to describe what is happening to the ranks of police services across the nation because of hiring freezes. In layman's terms, old farts are not being replaced with young whipper-snappers at the rate once experienced, and most of the police officers who come to your house now will have a little bit of grey around the temples, or in the ladies cases, crows feet around the eyes. Just think - in ten years you won't be able to call the police and get the young, fresh, handsome rookie whose biggest problem is how to get the cute secretary at his office to go out with him. Instead you'll get the old, somewhat stale, sagging senior cop whose biggest problem is haemorrhoids which were caused by sitting for too many years in a police car.

How does a cop know when he's getting too old?

• You've sat in the police car so long everything hurts, and what doesn't hurt doesn't work.

• The gleam in your eyes is from the sun bouncing off your summons folder.

• You feel like the morning after, but you were home in bed last night.

• All of the waitresses names in your little black book have been replaced with doctors.

• You get winded closing your uniform shirt buttons.

• Your children begin to look middle-aged.

• You finally reach the top of the promotional ladder, and it's leaning against the wrong wall.

• Your application to join a health club is turned down because you are a health risk.

• The only part of your body making dates with the cute waitresses with blue fever is your mind.

• Driving your police car during a rainstorm causes uncontrollable bladder urge.

• You look forward to a dull shift.

• You walk to the next call with your head held high - trying to get used to your bifocals.

• Your favourite part of the newspaper is "Today in History"!
• Your knees buckle but your gun belt doesn't.
• Your uniform shirt collar is 17, your uniform equipment belt is 44, and when you add these two numbers together they equal your golf handicap.

I'm not saying that I'm getting old but I went on a walk-through in a bar recently and two women were fighting over me. No, I'm serious! They were shoving each other and yelling, "No, you saw him first!"

"No, I didn't. You saw him first!"

Middle age spread happens a little faster when you have been sitting in a car for fifteen years. I drove to a local park the other day and was doing a check of the patrons when I stopped near the pool to watch the swimmers. I suddenly heard a woman's voice behind me.

"Johnny, that's not nice," she was saying to her son who was standing in my shadow. "Move over and let your sister in the shade too!"

*　　*　　*

Here is a list of the top five things you probably shouldn't say to a cop when you've been pulled over:

1) Shouldn't you guys be hanging out at the Blue Oyster or some other cop bar?

2) Tell me something guys, what are you doing out tonight? Isn't Robo Cop on at nine o'clock?

3) Be honest, you always wanted to be one of the Village People didn't you?

4) What are you guys doing in this neighbourhood? There's not a doughnut shop around for miles.

5) Why don't you stop pestering me and go find a pit bull to bother.

*　　*　　*

Some years back I worked for the Animal Control Unit as a Special Constable. I was called out of bed one night to attend at a motel in the seedier area of town. I was told by the dispatcher that a woman had died in one of the motel rooms and there was a dog inside who was defending the body. The police had requested my attendance to deal with the dog because it wouldn't let them into the room.

I gathered my mad dog gear up and in less than an hour I was standing in the parking lot of the motel. The place looked like a major crime scene. There were police cars all over hell's half acre and more cops than you could shake a stick at. I had actually been able to see the red and blues of the police cars five blocks away.

I remember thinking to myself, "Just what I need to be dragged out of bed for - to wrestle with a possessive pit bull or a Doberman. Why me?"

I spoke with the sergeant who was in charge.

"What we have here," he said, pointing to the upper level walkway which was crawling with cops crouching against the walls, "is a very vicious dog protecting the body of a deceased woman, possibly the owner. We have not heard movement for about an hour and a half now, but the first officer on the scene has determined that there is a dog of unknown breed in the room. It will be your job to enter the room first, secure the animal, and clear the way for our personnel. Be aware that if the animal attacks you, we will be forced to put it down immediately."

"Okay," I replied, opening the side of my truck and retrieving my heavy leather gauntlets. This sounded bloody serious and I wasn't about to get bit. I took my long pole with the slip loop and as a last thought I slipped on my leather ankle protectors. No chances; I hated getting tetanus shots.

The sergeant guided me to the room door on the upper walkway and ordered his men to clear the path. I felt like the conquering hero in an Arnold Schwartzenagger movie, but probably looked more like Goofy catching butterflies.

At the room door I paused and took a deep breath; my heart pounded and sweat broke out on my forehead. The constable at the door nodded at me and pushed the door open. I gathered my moxie and stepped across the threshold. I felt a rush behind me and two officers burst into the room with guns drawn for my protection.

There, sitting on the bed, was a quivering, trembling Yorkshire Terrier weighing all of about four ounces soaking wet.

*   *   *

I stopped a guy one day who was driving a pickup truck with a dealer plate on it. He was obviously using the truck for private business and was therefore illegally using the plate. When I finished with him I had issued him three thousand dollars worth of tickets, seized the dealer plate for evidence, impounded the truck and made the poor guy walk to a bus stop. He was not impressed with me at all.

Months later I was working a stop sign and a very pretty lady ran the sign. We struck up a conversation and after issuing her the ticket I suggested that we might have lunch. We ended up dating and today that lady is my wife.

Shortly after becoming engaged she invited me to her favourite aunt's house to meet the family. I accepted and we were having a great time playing billiards and having a few drinks in the rec room when I heard someone coming downstairs.

Her aunt called to me and said, "I'd like you to meet my son."

I turned and stuck out my hand and there was the guy I had written three thousand dollars worth of tickets to.

"Holy shit," I said, recognizing him instantly.

"Son-of-a-bitch," he replied with a grin,

"and that isn't all I called you that day."

*   *   *

Magistrate to the accused before deciding the outcome of the trial, "Do you have anything to say before I pass judgement upon you?"

"Yes, sir," replied the accused, "as God is my witness, I stand before you not guilty."

"Well," replied the magistrate, "in the unlikely event of your witness attending and giving evidence, case proved.   Fine is fifty pounds or three days. Next."

*   *   *

Life sometimes got dull walking the beat in the old days, so if we could think of something to liven it up a bit, we usually did it. I was assigned to the back alley detail in the downtown core and it was my job to walk all of the alleys. Another constable would start from the other end of the main streets and we would meet in the middle where we would stop for some conversation and a smoke.

I had a plan and I hurried my property checks to get to the meeting place ahead of my cohort. I climbed into a hotel garbage bin and found a very soggy box of kitchen garbage. I climbed the nearest fire escape and my intention was to drop the box of slop behind my partner, scaring the hell out of him and giving us a good laugh. I watched as he approached the end of the alley. I was in luck - he wasn't going to look up and see me.

He strode ever so slowly towards my position and I readied the slop bomb over my head. Just as he walked under the fire escape our patrol sergeant entered the alley. He came over to my partner and the two of them stood there talking and having a quiet smoke. If the sergeant caught me I would be on night shift for a year. I couldn't move. As a matter of fact I couldn't even put the box down because the fire escape would squeak. There I stood for the duration of their smoke with the box of garbage oozing out of its seems, running down my cheeks and filtering all the way to my armpits.

*　　　*　　　*

I got a call one night about a guy and a girl yelling and screaming upstairs from the complainant. I attended and waited outside with the complainant listening. We could hear a male and female but they didn't seem to be arguing. "They were really yelling and screaming before you got here," the neighbour insisted.

"I'll go and check on them," I said and

mounted the stairs.

I knocked on the door and a guy answered it, wrapped in a bath towel.

"Is everything all right here?" I asked, looking past him into the living room. A lady was just slipping on her housecoat and she too came to the door.

"Everything is fine, officer," he said with a questioning look on his face. "Is something the matter?"

"Well, your neighbour downstairs heard some yelling and screaming and wanted to make sure you were okay."

The man blushed. "I'm sorry to waste your time, officer," he said. "We were making love and I guess we get a bit noisy sometimes."

"I guess you do," I replied. "Maybe you should consider closing the windows in future."

I went back downstairs and the complainant was waiting for me on the sidewalk.

"Is everything all right?" she asked.

"Oh, yeah," I said, "it was just an in-to-mate moment, nothing to be concerned about."

"Oh, good," she said, stepping back to her own door. "For a moment I thought somebody was really getting it up there!"

* * *

The ambulance guys called us one night

to come and give them a hand looking for a drunk. We met them and they told us they needed to locate a guy on the main street somewhere who was very drunk and couldn't tell them where he was. Before responding to the call, one of the guys had slipped into their dispatch and taped the original. It went something like this:

"Ambulance service, what is your emergency?"

"I . . . uh . . . need a ambliance."

"What is the problem, sir?"

"I don't feel too good."

"Where are you, sir, what's your address?"

"I think I'm callin' frum uh pay phone."

"Before I can send an ambulance, sir, I need to know where you are. Can you see an address nearby?"

"Jus a minute," he replied and dropped the phone. There was silence for a few moments and then he came back on the line. "I'm at 45.9 Litre Street, right near a gas station."

*   *   *

He was a rookie in the late fifties and in those days there wasn't any academy training. You were given a gun and more or less learned as you went. My new partner may not have been cut out to be a policeman because he couldn't stand the sight of blood and cadavers nearly sent him into shock.

We received a call to investigate the welfare of a lady who had not been seen in over a week. Her neighbours were rather worried. We arrived at the house to find it locked up tight with papers and mail accumulated on the front step. Walking around the house we found a window that was slightly open. It was decided that I would boost my partner through the window so he could look around. He put one foot onto the gas pipe and I cupped his other in my hands. One, two, three and he was up and in. I heard a deafening scream from inside. At first I thought it was the old lady and we had scared her half to death. I was wrong. She was completely dead and my partner had landed on the bed right on top of her.

*　　　*　　　*

A police officer in London had arrested the accused for 'loitering with intent to commit an arrestable offence'. The offence required three overt acts and was most often used against persons found trying car doors. The defence counsel at trial did a sterling job of having the officer describe his exact position in relation to the accused. The result of his questioning determined that the police officer was standing around the corner of a building while the accused was doing his thing. The line of questioning continued something like this:

"So, what you're saying, officer, is that there was a brick building between you and my client?"

"Yes, sir."

"I think you would agree, sir, that you couldn't possibly see through these bricks to witness my client do anything, let alone what you have previously described."

"That's correct, sir. I couldn't have seen through the bricks."

The defence counsel grinned. He had laboured through this avenue of inquiry and built himself up to the final question which would surely acquit his client.

"Now, officer, please describe to the court how you could possibly have seen anything then?"

The policeman turned to the judge, leaned forward and cocked his head as if to peer around a corner, "Like this, Your Worship."

Now officer, please describe to the court how you could possibly have seen anything then!
Like this, Your Worship.
PEEK!

*   *   *

One night shift my partner showed up at work with six blanks for his service revolver. When I asked him what they were for he replied, "I'm going to load them into my gun and then sneak up on some unsuspecting constable, fire six rounds, and scare the piss out of him."

He laughed pretty hard at the thought of it and we hit the street. At about two o'clock in the morning we were checking out a park and drove under a long bridge. My partner decided he had to take a whiz. I stopped the car and he got out, leaving the six blanks on the seat.

I looked out of the corner of my eye and he was standing up against the wall taking a pee and reading the graffiti. I drew my gun, dumped out the live rounds, and slid the blanks in. Without making a sound I leaned out my car window and in quick, merciless succession fired off all six shots. My partner's wish came true. His blanks did scare the piss out of someone - himself. He jumped five feet in the air and spun around, penis in hand, just as I turned on the spotlight. There he stood, covered from ankles to adam's apple in piss.

*   *   *

Before joining the Bobbies in England I was an officer with the Royal Air Force and was quite used to commanding large bodies of men. Shortly after starting my career as a copper I received a call of a 'grievous bodily harm' offence and responded. When I arrived on scene I located a young college student who had been turned into a pile of Jello by a group of nine drunken soldiers on pass for the weekend. These soldiers, according to the victim, had just returned from a long stint in Northern Ireland where they had to exercise great restraint. He said they were very seasoned and it appeared they felt they did not have to exercise such great restraint any longer.

After arranging for medical attention for the victim and receiving descriptions from witnesses, I left in my patrol car to see if I could locate the assailants.

I hadn't driven far when I came upon a body of men strung out across the entire road, generally blocking everything in their path. I drove my car up quickly behind them, screeched to a halt and jumped from the vehicle yelling, "Where are you coming from?"

They turned in a group and one of the larger, more aggressive lads asked in a snarly, drunken voice, "What!"

I called up my best RAF officer's voice

and yelled back into his face, "I ASKED YOU WHERE YOU WERE COMING FROM! NOW SNAP TO ATTENTION WHEN YOU'RE TALKING TO AN OFFICER!!" He did and so did the rest of them.

"DON'T JUST STAND THERE," I hollered, "FALL INTO A SINGLE LINE ALONG THAT WALL."

They did.

I then carried out an impromptu inspection and noted that every one of them was slightly spattered with blood. I questioned them about the fight and they at first denied having any knowledge of it. I used my RAF officer's voice again and yelled, "YOU WOULDN'T BE LYING TO ME NOW WOULD YOU?"

"Yes sir, we are, sir," they replied as a group.

"Right then," I said, "fall in in three ranks and march the way back to the police station."

They did.

I marched them all right into the station and stood them at attention while I took each one separately into the charge room and dealt with them.

Some years passed and I emigrated to Canada. I made a trip home and went to my old station, and there I spied a young rookie constable who appeared to have about six hours on the department. I strode up to him and struck up a conversation. He looked a little suspicious until I said, "I used to be stationed here. I just wanted to drop in and see if any of my old colleagues were still about."

"What's your name," he said with some disinterest in the older policeman.

I introduced myself and he bolted to his feet.

"I know you!" he exclaimed, shaking my hand violently.

"How do you know me," I asked, rather surprised.

"You're the bloke what arrested two 'undered soldiers one night single 'andedly!"

* * *

I'm a female motorcycle cop and was riding bike one day when I responded to a call of some guy playing with himself on the bicycle path in a downtown park near the river. I rode onto the path and sure enough - there, right ahead of me, was this guy waving his lily around at everything that was moving. He didn't see me at all and I was able to ride right up to him without being noticed. I stopped my motorcycle inches from his back, reached out and grabbed his shoulder. He spun around, realized who I was, and bolted away from me. While I was putting the kickstand out on my bike, he was flapping his pecker all the way down the bank into the river.

He got caught in the current and I ended up having to call the fire department rescue boat to get him out. By the time they reached him he was turning blue he was so cold. You know it's true what guys say about cold water and their balls!

*   *   *

Police officers lead double lives verbally. The way they speak to each other and the way they speak to the public are most often very, very different. An officer was being interviewed by a news reporter at the scene of a boating accident in which a young girl had been injured. Prior to rolling the camera the reporter ran through the events with the officer.

The constable said words to this effect, "What happened was the little girl slipped on the dock trying to get into the boat and fell into the water."

"Great," said the reporter, "now when the cameras come on and I ask you the question, answer it just like you did and we'll be fine."

Moments later the camera was rolling and the reporter was telling the public where he was. He turned to the officer and asked, "Constable, can you tell us what happened here today?"

The constable sucked in his stomach, straightened his shoulders and said, "The young person allegedly misplaced her footing while attempting to board the floatation craft, and as a result, made an inadvertent entry into the water."

Even the average cop would have to sort that one out.

*   *   *

Here's another one from the civilian point of view.

I was having a party one night in the summer. It was very hot and late and I decided to go to bed while my roommate continued the party with her friends. I flopped down on top of the covers buck naked and tried to find some breeze from the open window. I soon dropped off to sleep.

While I was sleeping the police came to the party looking for someone who had a warrant out for them. They spoke to my friends but they wouldn't believe that the person they were looking for wasn't there. So my roommate asked them if they would like to search the house. They said yes and she led them through each room.

What I remember next was the overhead light coming on in my room, and waking up face to face with a cop who was just about as surprised as I was, if not more.

*   *   *

Yet another!

I was walkin' on the fairgrounds and really jerkin' around. Me and my friends were havin' max fun and not really watchin' what we were doin'. I dropped somethin' on the ground and like when I bent over to pick it up I hit my head on somethin' hard. I stood up real fast an' saw what I hit. Like, it was a cop's gun in his holster. Cool!

*   *   *

More civvi stuff!

I was getting a ticket one night for something I probably deserved. The cop was standing outside my car door and was writing in his ticket book. I looked out and noticed that his fly was down, so I told him. He didn't give me the ticket. Of course, I've gotten a few more tickets since then, and not one of those damned cops had their fly down. Had to pay every one.

*   *   *

Still more!

I was driving along the freeway with my husband and we were having a terrible argument. I had enough and I pulled the car over and told him to get out. He did and I drove off in a snit. About a mile down the road I had a brief moment of repentance and thought I should go back and get him. I stopped on the freeway shoulder and realized I couldn't turn around, so I got out of the car and started to walk back to where I had last seen him.

A police car went past me and stopped. The two cops got out of the car and started to walk towards me. I got real scared and started to walk a little faster. They walked faster too and then I started to trot. They trotted after me and I broke into a dead run. My heart was in my throat. I was thinking I don't know what I did but these guys really make me nervous. Finally one of them caught up to me and gently took hold of my arm to stop me.

"What did I do? What did I do?" I asked, with tears streaming down my cheeks.

"Absolutely nothing, ma'am," the young fellow replied. "We just noticed when we drove past you that the back of your skirt is caught in the top of your panty hose and we wanted to make sure you were all right."

*   *   *

One night while pounding the beat I noticed the back door of a business establishment had been broken in. As I approached, out sauntered the perpetrator. Upon spotting me he 'rabbited'. I chased him for several blocks and finally fired a shot over his head. Because I recognized him from previous run-ins a warrant was put out to pick him up.

He was arrested later at his home and brought to the station for questioning. He claimed to have been home all evening on the night in question. However, he had a scrape on his arm and the detective asked him what had happened.

"I fell down," he replied with a smirk.

"Isn't that where the constable shot you?" the detective asked.

"No," he replied, "he missed me!"

CHAPTER FIVE

The full moon . . . lover's light, artist's apocalypse, songster's symbol, bare buttocks. The moon has been a source of inspiration since time began. It has been regarded with fear, respect, love and curiosity throughout the ages. Its effect on mankind has been demonstrated time and again in religious ceremony, passage rites to adulthood, the singing of great love songs and the development of some police departments' policies.

Take for instance a recent policy presented by an unnamed department teaching its members how to deal with a vicious dog.

1) If a member during the course of his duties encounters a vicious dog, the member shall remain calm.

This is fine for the guy who wrote the policy, a little more difficult for the police officer who has just had his ankle gnawed, the ass chewed out of his uniform, his gun swallowed and his down-filled vest opened up making the yard look like a chicken plucking factory, by a pit bull who views him as the main course on the daily menu.

2) The member shall turn his body sideways and not stare directly into the dog's eyes.

Now, I don't know about you, but this dog has just impressed upon the cop that he is the hors d'oeuvres. Does the cop really want to turn around and allow him to select the next, more tender portion of his anatomy, into which it is his full intention to sink his teeth? I don't think so! And I don't know of any police officer who would be looking at the dog's eyes while he is being turned into a gnawing bone. Just ask any cop who has been attacked by a dog, "And what colour were the dog's eyes?" I guarantee he won't be able to tell you, but he can describe the three-foot-long teeth with impeccable accuracy.

3) The member shall speak to the vicious animal words of reassurance in calming tones.

Puuulllleeeeze! When a dog has just attached itself to the inside of your left thigh mere inches from the family jewels and is salivating like a Pavlov experimental canine, I truly believe the first words out of your mouth are going to be more in the line of, "HOLY

SHIT!, HELP!, GET OFF ME YOU SON-OF-A-BITCH!, OUCH!," or other expressions of a more normal nature. And I can guarantee the tones will not be calming.

I recall being involved in a foot chase one night in which the bad guy ran into an alley, leapt over a six foot wooden fence, and bolted through a back yard. Not wanting to lose the suspect I followed suit and scaled the fence right behind him. He was the lucky one. The doggy was sleeping when he jumped into the yard but was fully awake by the time he ran out the front gate. I was about in the middle of the yard when I heard the icy roar and felt the three-foot-long teeth sink into my ass. I immediately did my imitation of the Incredible Hulk, turning green from the pain, belching forth a primal scream and rescaling the six foot fence in a single leap. The dog, not happy with this hasty exit, let go of my ass and plunged its snapping teeth into the heel of my shiny, police issue boots. When the owner finally woke up and arrived to rescue me, he found me hanging upside down on the alley side of the fence, my gun laying in the long grass, flashlight illuminating the inside of his trash barrel and his dog dangling from my heel on the yard side still trying to consume my boot. He grabbed the dog by the collar and pulled him off, for which I was eternally grateful. But when the dog let go I fell head first into the metal trash can and rolled into the middle of the alley. I was trying desperately to extricate myself when the backup car crew arrived. Try living that one down! What stage was the moon in? How the hell would I know. I had my head stuck in a trash can!

However, if you think the moon doesn't have an effect on people, just try working with the police department, ambulance service, or emergency room at any hospital while the moon is full. Here are a few samples to be placed in evidence for your verdict.

* * *

"City Police, how may I help you?"

"I need a policeman."

"So do I, honey, but they're a little hard to find these days."

"No, I mean I really need a policeman."

"What's the problem, ma'am?"

"I had cable installed this morning and it's not working."

"The police don't do cable."

"They cut it off. And if they cut off my cable who knows what else they'll cut off."

"I'm sorry ma'am, the police don't do cable calls, you'll have to call the cable company in the morning."

"But I just need a man to come over here. He could protect me and my daughter from the cable cutters."

"I'm sorry, ma'am, I cannot dispatch a car to keep you company."

"Then why did you call me?"

"I didn't call you, ma'am, you called me."

"Stop phoning me or I'll call the cops!" Bang! The caller hung up.

I leaned around the corner of my telephone console and hollered at the sergeant, "What phase is the moon in?"

"Full," he yelled back.

"I thought so," I said.

*　　　*　　　*

"City Police."

"Hi. Can I tell you my story?"

"As long as it doesn't start with once upon a time, I guess you can."

"My buddy and I were drinking quite a bit last night and after we got pretty tipsy we took a taxi downtown. We went to that area."

"What area is that, sir?"

"You know, the one where girls make a living with their bodies."

"You went to a modelling agency?"

"No, no, no, we went to Firth Avenue."

"Oh, you picked up a hooker. I see."

"Anyway, we took her home with us, and you can imagine what happened next."

"Not in my wildest dreams, sir."

"Not in mine either. Anyway we fell asleep and when we woke up she was gone. So was the $1,200.00 from my dresser."

"So you want the police to come and take a theft report."

"No! I don't want the police involved at all! What I need to know is if there is some type of insurance company I can call who covers this type of thing. You know, something taken by hooker by crook!"

I said no and hung up. "What phase is the moon?" I yelled.

"Full," came the answer.

"Thought so!"

*　　　*　　　*

"City Police, may I help you?"

"A man was just here and had sex with me, then he faked his death. People have tried to kill me five times today. My house is bugged and I don't trust anyone! I can't use the pay phone because he keeps stealing my quarters. He tried to kill me in another city too. When I fall asleep men keep coming over and putting their hands inside my bra and underwear. I don't know what they're looking for. When I wake up there are men standing all around my bed and they want to have sex with me. I was at a friend's house last week and he must have put something in my drink, because I fell asleep and when I woke up I was groggy, and when I went to the bathroom I smelled medicine in my urine. I have to go now."

Click - she hung up.

"What phase is the moon?" I yelled to the sergeant.

"Full!" he yelled back.

"Thought so!"

*　　　*　　　*

"City Police."

"Hi. Can you tell me if your officers wear those instruments on their belts that send out a signal if they get into a horizontal position?" the lady asked.

"Yes, they do," I replied. "They are a safety feature which has saved many an officer's life."

"I'm not interested in saving someone's life! I want to strap one of those things to my husband's ass so I'll know the next time he's screwing around on me! Where can I get one!"

Enough about moons already. Back to the street where the action continues!

*　　　*　　　*

One of the places we used to use to escape the bitter cold while pounding the winter beat was a funeral home. The owner graciously left the rear door unlocked for us and we used to meet there quite regularly to have a smoke. One of the guys on our beat was afraid of the place and refused to go inside. This night it was particularly cold and we talked him into meeting us there for a quick smoke.

We got there ahead of him and my partner climbed into a casket. I closed the lid down and was leaning on it when the other guy arrived.

"Bloody cold, isn't it?" he said, tossing his hat on the casket lid and drawing a smoke from inside his winter coat.

"Damn right," I said, taking a deep drag on my own smoke.

"Got a light?" he asked, fumbling in his jacket pocket.

That was my partner's cue. He raised the casket lid a few inches, stuck his hand out with a lighter and lit it. I don't know if our comrade even opened the door before he went through it.

*   *   *

Drunks are the same the world over. Some rowdy, some friendly, some sorry, some happy. I remember being sent to a domestic call one night only to arrive and find one of the biggest and usually meanest drunks in the area standing in his ex-wife's apartment. I had dealt with him before and we had had a few good fights. The police always won but it usually took four or five of us and I was by myself. I opted for a different tack this time.

"What's the problem, sir?" I asked him.

He turned and looked at me with liquored eyes. "What did you call me?" he asked.

"Great," I thought, "can't even be nice to the guy, he's gonna fight anyway."

"I asked you what the problem was, sir."

"That's what I thought you said. Nobody ever calls me sir. I like you. Let's go. Have you got a paddy wagon or do I have to get handcuffed?"

"I have a paddy wagon," I said with notable relief.

We left quietly and I helped him into the back of the wagon. As I closed the door he was sitting on the metal seat waving at me with a silly grin. I waved back.

No sooner was I in the van when another call came in about a drunk trying to get into someone's house. I was only a block away so I volunteered. When I booked out I saw a guy standing between the houses with a two by four in his hands swinging wildly at the window. He saw me coming and ran behind the house. I stopped the van, bolted and chased after him. When I reached the back yard I found him sitting in a lawn chair on the deck as if nothing was wrong.

"The guy yer lookin' for jush went over tha back fensh," he said, still holding the two by four.

"Nice try," I said, grabbing the piece of wood and pulling it from his hands.

The fight was on. He came out of that chair like a wild cat, all teeth and nails and spitting and cursing. This guy was a lot more than I bargained for. I tried to pull my portable radio out of its holder but he just knocked it from my hand and kept climbing all over me. We tumbled backwards over a bike and he had me. He was on top of me with one hand on my throat, and with the other he found the two by four and had raised it over his head.

I was just going for my gun when he flew off me like his shorts were attached to a passing bus or something. I staggered to my feet and heard a single, solid and very loud, 'SMACK!' Out of the darkness came my friend the drunk from the domestic. He was dragging the butthead behind him like a rag doll.

130

"Nobody treats my friend like that," he said with a grin.

"How did you get out of the van?" I asked, rubbing my tender throat.

"Those doors aren't very strong," he said. "When I heard you in the fight I just gave it a good kick. I guess you'll be charging me with the damage, huh?"

"Not this time, buddy. I owe you big. Let's get this guy to the tank and I'll buy you a coffee."

"How about a beer?" he asked.

"Don't push it," I said.

*   *   *

Back to merry old England!

Over a period of service at one particular station you got to know all the local drunks. Most of them were friendly old boys with whom coppers shared a certain sort of relationship. I remember having sing-songs in the back of the station van on numerous occasions as the locals were loaded up and brought to the cells to spend a warm night.

One night I was posted to the van with a colleague and we set off in the hope of a busy Friday night. We soon came across a regular customer who was well past the point of looking after himself. We bundled him into the back of the van, and both agreed that it would be quicker and easier to drive him home rather than bother with all the paperwork of an arrest.

Asking him where he lived proved to be a five minute course on deciphering a drunken Irish accent. Eventually we managed a translation of 'Turty-Aide Chesterton Road.' I wrote in my notebook 38 Chesterton Road and off we went. Easy enough!

On arrival we helped him to the front door. He seemed to come around somewhat at this point and started saying, "I don live 'ere."

We questioned him again and he responded, "I tole yah, Turty-Aide Chesterton Road!"

"We're 'ere now," I said, "this is 38 Chesterton Road."

"I'm saree boys, I swear to Gawd I don live 'ere."

"C'mon Paddy, stop muckin' about an' go inside," I said.

By now we were getting very frustrated with this drunk. We thought we were doing him a favour and it seemed he just wanted to jerk us around. I even took his keys from his pocket and tried them in the door. They didn't fit and he wouldn't sway from his conviction that he lived at 'Turty-Aide'. Eventually we dragged him back to the van and set off for the station. Once he was safely put away and sleepin' like a leprechaun in his cell, I pulled out his local file to complete the arrest report. There on the form was his address, '30 A Chesterton Road.'

*   *   *

"Hello. Is this the police help line?"

"This is Victim Services. How may I help you?"

"I have something to report that is very urgent."

"Do you have a case number, sir?"

"No, I have to report and I have to talk to you."

I was beginning to think this may be serious and I should probably listen.

"Go ahead, sir."

"Yes, are you listening?"

"Please go ahead with your information. Are you all right?"

"No! The other night there was a serious violation on my dwelling abode. I arrived on my vehicular landing pad and found my chest that holds dead fauna material open and on its side in my front flora. My sitting utensils were strewn all about in the abode, my private body coverings were out of their containers, and my faecal commode had been uprooted from its anchor. I am distressed and I want you to send your footmen over to talk to me, to help me."

"SARG!" I yelled across the room.

"Yo," he replied.

"What phase is the moon?"

"Full."

"I thought so!"

Okay, okay. I had to slip one more moon story in for you!

*   *   *

Not every policeman is six feet tall and built like a wrestler. When I joined the force in 1957 I had the distinction of being the smallest guy on the job. I was five foot eight and weighed in at one-sixty. I took a lot of good natured abuse like the night I drew office duty, and when I went to help the first person, someone had placed a box there so I could see over the counter.

Then there was the bulletin which was posted in the locker room asking for volunteers to shoot gophers because Constable Doe needed a new buffalo coat.

I remember being sent to a bar disturbance one night, and when I got there, the guy was four times my size and not a happy drunk. I was going to wait for backup but he had different ideas. I managed to talk him down a bit and to convince him to let me handcuff him "for his own safety". After I got the first cuff on he changed his mind and decided it wasn't such a good idea after all. I had the one cuff on his wrist, and I was hanging onto the other for dear life with my fingers looped through it. He was trying to shake me off and I was flailing around like a pit bull on the end of a pork chop. I've never run so many miles without leaving a room in my life. By the time my backup arrived I was exhausted just from running back and forth.

Then there was the time I was working the arrest area, and two guys brought in a very, very large lady for being drunk and disorderly. In order to get her into the drunk tank I had to manipulate her up a narrow set of stairs. Things were going just fine until she tore my badge off with her bare hands, squashed it under her heel, and pinned me against the wall. The most embarrassing part was having to holler for help!

* * *

I was dispatching the downtown board on a very busy night. We had fights and domestic disputes and stolen cars and an accident on the go all at the same time. In the midst of all the mayhem I was notified of a robbery at a convenience store. It was my job to dispatch a car and get out as much information as I could on description of culprits and the crime vehicle as quickly as possible.

I was dispatching the location and a description of the bad guy when someone sent me a vehicle description. I continued with my dispatch, and at the same time was sorting the information cards to place them in order of importance. The car crew descending on the scene was asking me for a vehicle description in case they came across it leaving the area. Someone else was asking for a culprit description, and the duty sergeant wanted the address to attend in person.

I laid all the cards in front of me and stepped on the transmit pedal, a little frustrated by all the requests for information. But maintaining my cool I commenced giving the descriptions and location in an orderly fashion. When I got to the description of the car I was on a roll. I had them right under control now and they weren't going to frustrate me with more questions. I was cool!

"All units, the following is a description of the suspect vehicle in the armed robbery of the convenience store. (It was a late model Olds Cutlass.) All units be on the lookout for a late model, dark blue veal cutlet with damage to the right front fender."

It took hours for the smartass remarks

to settle down!

*   *   *

It was my first night on the job. I was excited because I had heard so much about night shift and the interesting calls you could go to and all the action. I was bristling when we left the office and my older, larger, somewhat laid-back officer coach detected it.

"I have an important job for you, so stay with me kid," he said.

I couldn't wait! Were we going to arrest a bank robber, or a serial killer, or a car thief? What was this important job he had for me? To think, only a week on the job and he trusted me already with important work.

He started the car, and we promptly drove to a very dark field, very far away from the office. He pulled into what looked like a gravel pit and shut the car off. Were we on a stakeout, were we going to meet some undercover guys and exchange some important info? What the hell was going on?

"All right," he said, releasing the seat latch and pushing it back as far as it would go. "Keep an ear to the radio for our call sign and let me know if anything breaks."

With that he dropped his chin onto his ample chest and almost immediately began snoring. It was pitch black. I couldn't see a damned thing and the radio was silent for a long, long time. After a while I began getting the nods myself and I fell into a deep sleep.

"Holy shit!" the voice burst into my ears. I tried to sit up but my head was pinned between the seat and the door post.

"Whunnhhh," was the best I could come up with because my mind was still asleep and my lips were squashed to the side.

"It's ten past seven in the morning and we were supposed to be in by seven. We're gonna get shit!"

He grabbed the seat latch and jammed the seat forward. Now my head was quite securely pinned against the door post. My ears were folded back on both sides and my nostrils were stretched wide like a raging bull.

It took me quite a few blocks to extricate myself, and when I did I discovered that I had drooled on my new uniform shirt. We arrived at the office and he disappeared, leaving me to turn in all the equipment. I went to the sergeant and he was looking at me rather strangely.

"Is something wrong?" I asked, my knees trembling.

"No, no. Not at all," he replied, raising one eyebrow.

"Whew! I got away with it. I'm home free," I thought to myself.

I wandered up to the locker room and

changed my clothes. I wanted to freshen up a bit before I left to go home, so I went to the bathroom sink. As I leaned over I looked into the mirror and there, big as life, was the complete and recognizable imprint of the seatbelt buckle with the words 'GM - Safety First.'

*   *   *

It's a well known fact that British police officers are unarmed. I always felt a little safer carrying my issue truncheon, however, my partner would constantly leave his in his locker. One late turn shift we were on regular traffic patrol when a call was broadcast to a nearby address - 'suspects on premises, a break and enter in progress'.

We were the first unit there and it was obvious that the venue had been broken into. It was, in fact, a lawyer's office and we both cautiously entered the building. The front door opened to a long flight of stairs leading to the first floor offices. Once inside we split up, my partner doing one side of the building while I did the other. As I looked around I could see drawers pulled out and contents spread over the floor. I thought it strange at the time that two small refrigerators had been opened as well.

It wasn't too long before I heard a scream from across the hall, and with my heart in my mouth, I lunged around desks and chairs to reach my colleague, whom, I suspected, was in severe distress. As I entered the room from where the shouts had come I shone my light in the direction of a voice. To my chagrin I was presented with my partner holding a male suspect at bay with the cleaners broom.

The man was extremely large and was standing with his hands in the air. In his grasp was a bottle of Glenfiddich Scotch.

"All right, Guv," he said, "all right. I'll give yuh no trouble."

He pointed to the bottle of Scotch. "Would yuh mind, it's bin a lengthy day?"

He could have torn us apart with his hands and we weren't in much of a position to refuse him a quick sip. He tipped the bottle and downed about four inches of the contents before he stopped. Then he set the bottle on the desk and said, "I'm yers, let's go."

Being in traffic we had no cage in the area car so he just sat in the back and chatted merrily to us along the way.

"I've just been released from servin' seven years fer manslaughter," he said with some concern.

I was getting somewhat concerned myself.

"Don' take this personal but yuh know it's rather embarrassin' bein' set upon by a couple o' traffic coppers."

"Tell you what," I said, "let's strike a deal. You don't rip our car apart and we don't tell who arrested you."

"An' you won' tell nobody that yer partner 'ere 'eld me with a broom 'andle?"

"You've absolutely no worry about that," I said.

*   *   *

Recently an anonymous caller came forth with information that a group of persons had gathered together for terrorist reasons. He was of one nationality and they were of another, and he had been privy to a conversation in which this group of four young men had openly discussed 'shooting down the airplane'. Such conversations are not to be taken lightly by the police, and as a result of some quick phone calls, the group of four was determined to meet on a regular basis. It was decided that the potential for a threat existed.

A team of investigators was called together, targets were identified for undercover surveillance, and court orders were received to permit wire taps on the phones of these four suspects. In less than four days the entire operation was in full swing, and files began to grow rapidly as information poured in.

The only problem was the wire tap. All four of the men spoke little English on the phone, and as a result, a translator had to be located to transcribe the tapes of the wire tap. One was hired and he was given an office to himself with everything he needed to transcribe the tapes as they rolled off the recorder. He listened intently for a number of hours and made furious notes on the conversations. He was nearing the end of the second tape, and a number of the high-ranking police officers assigned to catch the would-be terrorists gathered to study his results.

The translator suddenly came upon the phrase they had been waiting for - shooting down the airplane - as clear as day in the dialect. He looked at the men standing over him in anticipation. He gazed into each of their eyes intently and quickly began to smile widely. Soon he began to chuckle, and ultimately he had to take his headphones off to roar with laughter.

The police officers were amazed at his behaviour and regarded him with some disdain. Catching terrorists was not funny business. When he was able to control his fits of guffawing he managed to blurt out, "You don't have a bunch of terrorists here. What you have is a bunch of young men bragging."

"What's so funny about that?" one of the officers asked him.

"In my language," he said, wiping the tears from his eyes, "the term 'shooting down the airplane' is another term for male masturbation! And if they can bring down a plane with that, they deserve credit, not jail!"

*   *   *

The courtroom drama was unfolding before the judge. The accused sat expressionless in the prisoner's box, the defence lawyer adjusted fine-rimmed glasses on a bony nose as he poured over his scrawled notes, and the police officer waited patiently on the witness stand for the next question.

"Constable," the lawyer said, not raising his eyes from the paper he was scrutinizing, "did you make notes on this incident?"

The constable replied, "Yes, I did."

"And," the lawyer continued, turning a dog-eared page with nicotine stained fingers, "did you refer to those notes today before you came to court?"

"No, I did not," said the constable, hooking his thumbs into his equipment belt and performing the police officer's secret one finger check to ensure that his fly was zipped to the top.

"Well then," continued the lawyer, tugging at his earlobe and straightening his tie in two closely executed and practiced moves, "did you refer to them recently?"

"No, I did not," the constable said again,

somewhat more relaxed at confirming that his fly was not down and he was not displaying his multicoloured boxer shorts to the court-room.

The lawyer, sensing victory, but not wanting to rock the boat too violently just yet, pursued the line of questioning. He looked at the officer over the rim of his wire framed Vicente glasses, pulled them yet a little lower on his nose for effect, and asked, "Constable, have you referred to these notes at all since the time of this incident?"

The constable remained calm, flicked the corner of his moustache with the back of his forefinger, and replied, "No, sir, I have not."

The lawyer dropped the file to the table, removed his glasses with whip-like speed, and pointed them at the officer. "Constable, maybe you can explain to the court then, how it is that if you made notes on this incident, which took place last year, and you have never again referred to those notes to refresh your memory, you can recall the events so clearly!"

"Yes, sir I can . . ." the officer started.

"Please do!!!" the lawyer spat sarcasti-cally.

"In all my twenty-three years as a police officer this was the most dangerous case of dangerous driving I have ever witnessed."

The lawyer spun on his heels and yelled at the judge, "Your Honour, Your Honour, I demand the last remark be stricken from the record! It is an opinion and is prejudicial to my client!!"

The judge leaned over his own note file, pulled his glasses down, and smiled at the lawyer. "You asked the question, mister," he said, "you live with the answer."

CHAPTER SIX

There is a saying, "Old cops never die, they're just summoned to higher courts." Well, okay, I made it up but it could be a saying now! Let's take a look at a few more of the "Greying of the Blue - you know you're getting old when" truisms.

"How does a cop know when he's getting old . . . continued."

•   After painting the police bar red, you have to take a long rest before applying the second coat.
•   Picking up the radio mike to respond to a call wears you out.
•   You want to bust a dirt bag just because he called you "old timer".
•   You forget little things, like today wasn't

your day off and you were supposed to be on shift an hour ago.

- You become intolerant of supervisors who are intolerant.
- The best part of your day is over when the alarm clock goes off.
- Burning the midnight oil starts at 9:00 P.M.
- Your back goes out more than you do.
- You answered a call where a fortune teller had been ripped off by a client and she offered to read the lines in your face.
- The little old grey haired lady you helped across the busy street on shift today . . . was your wife.
- You head to your favourite on-duty eating spot to flirt with your favourite waitress and enjoy your favourite food - a late night steak - but when you sink your teeth into it . . . they stay there.

Thinking on your feet is an art similar to riding a bicycle - once you learn you never forget. As you age and mature you become somewhat more adept at it; or you just increase the size of your mouth so you can get both feet in at the same time.

I transfered to an administrative position with the Service while maintaining my rank as constable. When I left my partner on the street to assume the new desk job he gave me a gift - a model of a Tyrannasaurus Rex standing in slime and eating something. His advice, "Don't forget who you are working with now and what they can do to you." I took his advice to heart and my dinosaur to my new desk.

My new boss came to greet me and immediately noticed the model next my blotter. He picked it up, examined it, and looked at me with a raised eyebrow.

"What does this represent?" he asked, holding the plastic animal out to me.

I plucked it from his hand, replaced it on my desk and said with a grin, "It's a gift from my partner to remind me that we were the senior car crew in the zone when I left."

I hope he accepted the explanation, but the cat's out of the bag now! Speaking of which - here's a great story with a different twist on that old saying.

*   *   *

I had made arrangements for a suspected bad guy to come with me to take a polygraph test. Out of courtesy, and to ensure he would be there, I went to his house to pick him up. When he answered the door he immediately began making excuses and trying to worm his way out of the test. I was determined he was going to go with me because I was convinced he was guilty as hell and I wanted to prove it.

While we were having this brief and subdued discussion at the door I was watching his little black kitten romping around the living room. It jumped at a string hanging from the coffee table, arched its back, rolled over and disappeared under the couch. I thought to myself, "I bet you could tell me a thing or two about this guy if you could talk." The thought no sooner was finished when the little kitten leaped out from under the couch with a small plastic bag between its front paws. As I watched, the kitten bounded towards me, flinging the bag from side to side and finally flipping it into the air. It came to land right at my feet.

I noticed the look of horror on the bad guy's face as I bent over to pick the bag up. It was full of marijuana. I held the bag in my hand, looked him in the eye and said, "Well, this is different, the cat let the bag out! Get your shoes, you're under arrest."

*　　　*　　　*

At the end of each trial both the crown and the defence are permitted to address the judge with final remarks. It is during this time that the crown prosecutor will summarize the case and place his request for incarceration before the judge. When he has completed this task it is the defence lawyer's turn to address the bench and try to keep his client out of jail if he can.

The case had been a lengthy one and the judge was obviously considering some healthy time for the accused. The lawyer had not done well in his defence and he was desperate in his plea to reduce or eliminate the time his client would have to serve. He could tell from the disinterest displayed by the judge that even this part of his plea was not going well.

In frustration he finally threw his hands up in the air and stated, "Your Honour, I can at least say this about my client: His record would not be half as bad as it is if the police would only stop catching him!"

*   *   *

It was a very, very hot day. I was working day shift and had gone from accident to accident without a break. Most of my time was spent standing out in the sun taking statements from witnesses and drivers, noting damage to the vehicles, and making sense out of the skid marks on the road. I was so busy that I didn't pay attention to what my body was telling me and I suffered a mild heat stroke.

I arrived at the next call and one of the drivers was a very pretty young lady. I was standing on the road dealing with her when all of a sudden my stomach turned from the heat. Without warning I started to throw up and didn't want to do this in front of her. I turned my back and the only thing I could think of to do was grab my hat. I was so embarrassed! I placed the upturned hat on the ground and tried to continue the interview as best I could. She could tell I was rather sheepish.

"It's okay," she said with a smile, "my boyfriend doesn't like this perfume either."

*   *   *

Sometimes the radar cop can help you out. I was working a particularly busy location one day and stopped a young lady for exceeding the speed limit. When I took her license I noticed her last name and it rang a bell with me. I went back to the police car and rummaged through my summonses, and sure enough there was one there for a guy with the same, unusual last name.

When I returned to her car to give her the ticket I asked her, "Excuse me, but are you somehow related to Mr. So and So?"

"Why yes," she replied, "that's my husband. Do you know him?"

"Not really," I said, "but I did stop him for speeding here about five minutes ago."

"Oh, thank you, thank you," she said with glee. "Picture this. When I get home he will sit down to supper and ask me what's new. I'll tell him I got a speeding ticket and he'll call me a stupid woman. Then I'll ask him what's new. I can hardly wait! This is the best ticket I ever got!"

*　　　*　　　*

In Canada an accused's criminal record may not be brought out during a trial unless the accused does so himself.

I was walking the beat one day and as I passed a rather dirty, greasy young man sitting on some steps, he flicked a cigarette butt onto the sidewalk right in front of me. I pulled out my summons folder and approached the guy.

"If you don't have fifty bucks to waste, I'd suggest you pick that butt up and dispose of it properly," I said.

"Piss off, " he replied, and stood to his feet. He strode to the butt with an attitude and kicked it into he gutter.

Needless to say, I wrote him a summons for littering and went on my merry way.

The guy plead not guilty and the court

case finally came up. I was on the stand and gave my evidence as to the events which had taken place that day. When I was finished the judge asked the accused, who was still dressed in the same dirty jean jacket, torn jeans, and food-stained t-shirt he was wearing months ago when I wrote him the ticket, "Do you have any questions for the constable?"

"Yes, I do," he replied, jumping to his feet. "I wanna know why this cop called me a sex offender, child molester, and a piece of garbage!"

"Don't ask me," said the judge, "ask him."

"Well," said the accused, sticking his chin out and attituding all over me. "Why did you call me a sex offender, a child molester, and a piece of garbage?"

"Prior to writing you the summons for littering I ran your name for record and warrant," I said, knowing that was as far as I could go without causing a mistrial for blurting out the guy's record.

"Just what did you come up with?" the guy asked, expecting to take me to task, but only opening the doors for me to legally enter his record into the trial.

"When I ran your name," I continued, with the slightest twinge of a smile, "I determined that you had a record for sexual assault and child molestation. In my mind that makes you a piece of garbage."

The bad guy looked at the judge for some help.

The judge simply made a note on the file, and without raising his head, asked, "Any more stupid questions for the constable?"

*   *   *

The TAC Team! The Elite! The bigger-than-life, glorious-prestigious-assignment-filled-by-macho-guys-who-weight-train-harder, shoot-better, get-into-the-action, and dress-cooler-than-anyone-else-on-the-department department.   I was so excited about being accepted onto the team and I couldn't wait for my first assignment. My adrenalin was high just getting dressed for the first time in my dark coloured TAC uniform, special issue boots, cool looking TAC pants and ball cap. I was ready to enter the inner perimeter of the next big weapons call and save the fair maiden who was being held captive by the evil bad guy.

Our first call of the day was to assist with a homicide. We arrived on the scene and I expected to be given a task befitting my new uniform. Would we be hunting for the suspect? Identifying the murder weapon? Possibly defusing a bomb he may have left behind? NOT!

The poor victim had been stabbed to death

and we were to help locate the knife. Our assignment was to check every garbage can and dumpster within a four block radius of the scene. It was a very hot day and in no time at all my nice, new, clean, cool uniform was covered in rotting vegetables and discarded restaurant food. So much for the exciting task!

But all was not lost. Soon a witness stated that she had seen the suspect running near the river and throwing something into the water. At last a decent assignment! We were to suit up and dive in the river to recover the weapon. Now I would get a chance to really do my stuff! I love to dive!

In an hour we were at the location and I was ready for action. We rigged a rope attached to a dinghy and a tether to stop us from being pulled down river by the strong current. The dinghy was attached to a pulley system which spanned the river with officers on each side. I was to tie my wrist to a cinch on the downstream side of the dinghy and they would pull me back and forth across the turbulent water while I searched the bottom for the weapon.

I made the knot, slipped my hand through the loop, and slipped into the icy stream. Now I was in my element and I knew I was going to find the knife. The average diver on the TAC Team would stay in the water for about five minutes and then had to be pulled out after fighting the current. It didn't take long to exhaust yourself. The signal to be pulled out was to bob to the surface and raise your arm.

It wasn't long after I entered the water that I realized I hadn't tied the cinch properly and I wasn't able to bob to the surface. In the standard five minutes I was competely exhausted, and try as I might I could not get to the surface to signal the crew. Minute after minute they dragged me back and forth across the rocky bottom of the river. I bounced over shopping carts, tires, rubber boots and big rocks. I was on my back, my side, my head, and try as I did I could not make my body float to the surface. My arm felt like it was being pulled out of its socket. Finally I could struggle no more and I just collapsed.

The guys on the shore must have felt a change in the tension or something because they decided it was time to haul me out. They pulled the dinghy ashore and it took two guys to lift me out of the water. I lay on the rocks, unable to even lift my hand to release my air tank.

The sergeant strode over to me and sat me up. I went right on over and fell on my face. "Hold on," he said. "You were down there for twenty minutes. An admirable job, but let's let someone else go back in."

"Okay," was all I could say. Little did

he know that I failed knot tying in Cubs. So much for the elite, macho, and keen first day with the TAC Team.

*   *   *

A 9-1-1 call came in and when the officer answered there was dead silence on the other end of the line. We were dispatched to the address to determine what the nature of the emergency might be. When I went to the door and rang the bell, the lights in the house flashed. This was my first hint that something was wrong. The person who answered the door was deaf, and he was flapping his hands at me in sign language so quickly I had no idea what he was trying to get across.

I stepped into the house and was met by a lady who was also deaf, and she started waving her hands at me. The guy must have understood her because he jumped between her and me and flapped his hands violently. She pushed him aside and began waving her arms wildly. He shoved her aside and did the same.

Drawing on all my training, I took out my notebook, tore out a page and wrote furiously. When I was done I passed the note to them. They read it and looked at me in amazement.

It said, "Both of you stop yelling at me

or I won't listen any more."

It was all I could think of, but it worked.

*　　　*　　　*

DUMB CRIMINAL ALERT!

How about the guy who phoned 9-1-1 to make an obscene phone call.

*　　　*　　　*

DUMBER CRIMINAL ALERT!

Then there were the two guys who broke into a house at Christmas time and opened all the presents. One of them was a Polaroid camera and they took pictures of each other opening the gifts under the tree. When they fled the scene, they left the pictures behind, developing in fine style on the kitchen table.

*　　　*　　　*

REALLY DUMB CRIMINAL ALERT!

Or how about the guy who stole his girl-friend's car after an argument with her. He drove the car into a tree and then left a note on the front seat. "Dear Betty, please tell the cops I didn't do this, okay. Love, John."

*   *   *

EVEN DUMBER CRIMINAL ALERT!

Then there was the guy who was suspected of robbing a convenience store. The police had a photo of him from the surveillance camera and he was pictured holding a sawed-off shotgun with a taped handle. When the bad guy was tracked down, he decided to prove his innocence by refusing to talk to the police, but provided a recent picture of himself for comparison to the surveillance photo. Of course he had changed his appearance a great deal. When the police enhanced the photograph they were able to identify the butt of the shotgun sticking out from under his couch. Jail time!

*   *   *

STILL DUMBER CRIMINAL ALERT!

I like the one about the bad guy who was photographed by a surveillance camera, and knowing this to be the case, altered his appearance to beat the charge. When he showed up in court with his 'new look' a detective working on a string of other robberies recognized the 'new look' as an 'old look', and busted him from photographs two years old.

*   *   *

DUMB DEE DUMB DUMB!

Then there was the guy who broke into a house and emptied the liquor cabinet as a last kick at the cat when he was leaving. He had packed all of the removable belongings into the victim's van and fled into the night. Some hours later he was arrested, passed out behind the wheel of the stolen van from having consumed far too much of the stolen liquor.

*   *   *

STRANGE BUT TRUE!

A transvestite bad guy used to get his jollies breaking into women's apartments and stealing their clothes. He took the booty home and would then take pictures of himself adorned in various ladies attire. I guess he just couldn't resist the temptation and he sent one of the pictures to an adult magazine. The magazine printed the picture, and as a result, the guy was located and arrested. He was wearing distinctive clothing from three different B and E's. (Now I won't hazard a guess as to how this picture was discovered by police in an adult transvestite magazine!!)

*   *   *

JUST PLAIN STUPID CRIMINAL ALERT!

How about the bad guy who knocked the ice cream boy from his bicycle-style ice cream cart and fled with the vehicle. The cart was found a short distance away with the bad guy's pants caught in the chain of the sprocket. He had been unable to extricate the pant leg from the chain so decided to peel them off and run. What he omitted to do was remove his wallet from his pocket before fleeing.

*   *   *

For those of you who have never had the wonderful experience of receiving a violation ticket in the mail as a result of committing an offence in front of a Multanova camera, allow me to explain. This is a camera that is hooked directly to a police van (and, some would say, directly to the city's bank account) and it takes pictures of you and your vehicle while you think the police aren't around. Gotcha! There are many stories associated with the Multanova camera and some of them are beginning to surface as classics. Here is a sampling of the few I have received in the recent past:

*　　　*　　　*

I was assigned to what I thought was going to be the most boring detail of my life - Multanova camera. When my sergeant told me all I had to do was sit on the side of the road and make sure nobody ran off with our $60,000.00 camera for eight hours, I figured, great - now I'm a babysitter for a piece of equipment. My attitude changed soon after when I realized that people do very strange things when they think no one is watching them.

Lots of people yell at themselves. I recall seeing a guy who was driving down the road screaming and hitting the dashboard of his car. He was by himself so I have no idea who he was fighting with. Lots of people sing and act out the songs too. I saw a lady, obviously with the radio up full, dancing in her seat and singing into a hairbrush like a microphone. We see everything from the proverbial nose nugget prospectors, to brassiere adjusters, mobile domestic disputes, and scintillating sex behind the wheel.

When we have completed the day's photographing we turn the film in to be developed at our Identification Section and wait for the results. Some of them have been hilarious. I recall seeing one of a car speeding along with the trunk lid partly open and the handlebars of a bicycle hanging out. When we blew up the picture to read the plate number we could also see the guy in the trunk holding the bike so it wouldn't fall out.

Then there was the picture I got back of the two beauties in the trunk of a car kneeling and baring their breasts to the camera as the vehicle sped away. They had their small shirts draped over the plate of course.

But my all-time favourite was a letter I received from an irate person who was the recipient of a Multanova speeding ticket. He was obviously upset but maintained a sense of humour. I can't reproduce the letter, but the contents came with a photograph of the offender and went something like this:

To Whom It May Concern:

Last week I received a notice in the mail that you had a picture of my car speeding on such-and-such street at such-and-such time on such-and-such date. Along with the letter was a ticket for speeding. I thought that since you were able to take a picture of my car speeding I would also send you a picture of me writing out the cheque for the fine. (There was no cheque in the envelope!)

*   *   *

This is a classic, and I know it has been told to have happened in every department in the world, but here it is just because it's so damned funny:

I was driving through a playground zone on my way home from work last week when I saw a police van with a speeder camera sitting in the area. I checked my speed and was doing the limit in the playground zone as I proudly drove past the van. To my amazement the flash went off as I drove past. I remember thinking, "There must be something wrong with his radar, I know I was not speeding." I decided to test out my theory and I rounded the block. With great deliberation, I drove past the van a second time, now travelling five kilometers per hour under the limit. To my amazement the camera flashed again. I couldn't believe it! This guy must have really screwed up his settings. I recall laughing and going around the block a third time. I drove past the van once again, this time ten kilometers per hour under the limit, and sure enough, FLASH!!! "Ha, ha," I thought to myself, "am I going to have a hay-day with this cop in court!"

I knew it would take about a week and sure enough the tickets finally arrived. With a great smirk I tore open the envelope and there they were - three tickets - for not wearing my seatbelt!!!

*   *   *

I set up the radar camera on a main road in the same spot for a week at a time. The first morning in my new spot a car came through the camera like a starship in warp drive. I just chuckled, thinking the owner would be very surprised when the sizeable ticket arrived. However, the next morning at about the same time he came through the radar spot again, this time faster than the day before.

After he came through even faster on the third day I decided I should enlist the help of a few of my cohorts and try to catch this guy before he killed someone. We set up with a couple of unmarked vehicles and waited. Like clockwork he arrived on the scene, this time doing two and a half times the speed limit. I radioed to the unmarked cars and they were able to pull him over without incident about three blocks away.

I uprooted the camera and drove to where they had him stopped and were just removing him from his vehicle. He was being very cooperative, and in fact was grinning quite widely.

"What are you trying to do?" I asked as

they placed him into handcuffs. "You must have known I was there, you've been past me four times now!"

"Oh, I knew you were there all right," he replied with an even wider grin.

"Well," I continued, "if you knew I was there, why in God's name would you continue to fly past me like a low flying jet?"

He continued to smile. "The owner of the vehicle is the one who gets the ticket, right?" he asked.

"Yes," I said, "it is sent out to the registered owner of the vehicle whether or not they were driving at the time."

"And they are completely responsible for the ticket, right?" he said.

"Right," I confirmed.

"Good!" he said. "My wife left me for another guy last month and she has just taken me to the cleaners for everything I own. She took the house, both cars, the kids and my business. I told her that I needed a vehicle to go and look for work and she loaned me hers. That oughta teach her!"

*   *   *

When a police officer arrives on the scene of an accident, they have many duties to perform including saving lives if necessary, tending to the injured, directing traffic, protecting the scene, and gathering evidence for any charges which may result. Part of the evidence gathering duty includes taking statements from drivers and witnesses. These statements, combined with the physical evidence of skid marks, debris, gouge marks and such, are the tools an officer has to use to make decisions in the field. With that in mind, I would like you to try and decipher some of these actual collision statements received from various sources across the nation. This is a test. You are the officer at the accident scene. Read each statement carefully and then see if you can tell what happened. These statements are unaltered except for locations and names which may identify the persons.

*   *   *

"I was parked on the corner of Smith Street and Jones Avenue wanting to get out of my car. I looked over my left shoulder and noticed a truck was travelling more toward the middle of the street and therefore I had lots of room to open the driver's door of my car. Looking again to the front of my car not noticing any other vehicles I just opened my door approximately twelve inches when the impact accurate for some reason the truck whose very close to my car hit my door with his passenger door."

*   *   *

A man was refusing to write a statement as the driver of a vehicle involved in a collision. I informed him that he must write a statement or be charged under the Highway Traffic Act for failing to do so. Reluctantly he took the pad from me and scribbled the following:

"I was in the police car to report the accident I was in. I was told I had to write this but I don't want to say what happened because they might blame me for the accident I was in."

*   *   *

"I said are you ok they said yes. I was come from the right line and they desedet to come from the other line because there is another line on the street because there is two lines there were come from the other line and they were coming first. I will explain to my insurance."

*   *   *

"I park in the right side of the street. I try to pull out from that place toward another street and I blind spoted a blue car and I hate the passenger."

173

Have you been sleuth enough to figure out who is going to get the ticket for the accident yet? I thought not. I have a few more of these gems but I'll save them for later. Time for a short pee break and we'll get on with the next chapter.

CHAPTER SEVEN

Bloopers have been going on since the dawn of police work. Here is the oldest one I have received. My apologies to the author (whom I do not know) and I take no claim to this particular story, however, it really is hilarious:

Before the turn of the century the Old West was not a place for the faint of heart. It was also not a place for some performers to make claims they might have trouble keeping. A certain magician was in a small town and had raised enough excitement with his claims that his safety was in jeopardy that the town sheriff decided to attend his performance.

He had told his audience that he would catch bullets in his teeth. What he hadn't told them was that he had hired an assistant who was going to fire blanks at him and he would in turn spit out slugs hidden in his mouth.

As the performance got under way the magician stood bravely in front of the awed crowd, and revelled in the hush which descended upon them as the assistant took aim. Suddenly the silence was broken as a drunken cowboy burst from the audience and drew his six gun. "Catch this one!" he yelled, staggering to the stage and pointing his gun at the magician. Just as the gun went off the sheriff struck the man's arm with his fist and the bullet went astray. The drunken cowboy went off to jail and the terrified magician went off to reconsider his act.

While we're on the topic of history, police work has been in my family for a long, long time. Apparently my great-grandfather was the first police chief of Owen Sound, Ontario. I remember how my grandfather used to tell me stories about his Dad and his police work in the early days of Owen Sound. Now we're talking the late 1800s here folks!

One of my favourite stories was about the deputy my great-grandpa hired to help him out one summer when things were getting a little hectic. This deputy, we'll call him Jake,

Pirate Per's
Polular
Performances

was reminiscent of "Festus" from Gunsmoke and "Gomer Pyle" from Andy of Mayberry. Now you just know with a combination like that things are bound to happen.

Jake was a bit of a drinker on the weekends, and one night after duty he rode his horse to the local saloon to quaff a few brews before retiring. While he was inside mingling with the crowd, a few of the patrons went out to the hitching rail and turned the saddle around on his horse. They cinched it up tight and then sneaked back inside.

The next morning my great-grandpa met up with Jake who was walking on the main street. He had had so much to drink the night before that he was still quite intoxicated.

"Jake, where's your horse?" he asked, knowing that Jake very seldom went anywhere on foot.

"Oh, I had a bad time last night, Percy," said Jake, pulling his hat from his head and twisting it like a dishrag.

"Tell me what happened," said Percy, dismounting and showing genuine concern.

"Well, you know I likes to have a few drinks now 'n then, but only off duty! Well, I went over to the saloon fer a couple and I guess I got to talkin' and had a lot more than a few. Matter of fact, Percy, to be honest I was real drunk. But the worst was that when I come outta the bar sumbody had cut the

178

head off my horse. I had to stick my hand down his throat and guide him all the way home!"

You see, things don't change much over the centuries. Here we are, a hundred years later, still providing protection and service to the public, ar ar ar!

*   *   *

It's time to take a quick shot at our friends in the Fire Department. The police have observers come with them sometimes while on shift and it's called having a "ride-a-long". What would the Fire Department call it if they had someone observe them at work - "a sleep-over!" It's a joke guys, a joke - don't take me off your response list, please!

Okay, one more shot at them. I recall being at a multiple vehicle collision one winter where two vehicles had ruptured their gas tanks and the contents were spilling onto the road under the other cars. I called for the Fire Department to attend and hose down the area, which they did with great expertise. Upon arrival at the scene it was the duty of one of their members to ensure that nothing could cause an explosion. There really was a lot of gas around! As I watched, the fireman retrieved a pair of huge cutters from his pumper and began quickly making his way amongst the damaged vehicles, raising the hoods and cutting the battery cables to prevent a spark from igniting the gasoline. He was working feverishly and obviously got a little carried away. Before I was able to yell at him he pried open the hood of an unmarked police car and cut the battery cables. Oops!

I was recently told by the paramedics that they used to get into the fray with the police as well. We would do things like calling them out to a particularly dirty drunk who had passed out. It was obvious that this person had urinated and defecated in his pants, and it also became obvious that this was more than a drunk, it was a collapse and we needed an ambulance to transport! The paramedics arrived and gave that look of great disgust at our angelic faces as they treated this rather messy person. Invariably, because the person was unconscious, they would have to transport to the hospital. We followed them over in our car and chuckled all the way as we watched the paramedic inside gasping for air all the way to the hospital.

When we got to the hospital we deliberately made ourselves scarce until they had the patient booked in. By the time we returned to the emergency area the ambulance crew was gone on another call. We breathed a sigh of relief and strode out to our police car. There it was, filled to overflowing with open bags of dirty diapers from the nursery.

*　　　*　　　*

A young rookie lawyer (yes, they are raw meat too!) was eager to make a good impression in court. When his time came to cross examine the medical examiner in the matter of a fatal accident, he arose from his seat and approached the witness stand. He spoke with confidence and looked the M.E. in the eyes.

"Sir, could you please tell the court how many autopsies you have performed on dead people?"

The witness stated with as much confidence, "All my autopsies have been on dead people, sir."

A recess was called to allow the court to regain its composure.

*　　　*　　　*

As a radar cop, I have been given "the finger" a number of times, but one time sticks out in my mind above all. It was a Saturday morning and I had driven my motorcycle to one of my favourite locations to catch a few speeders. This was a particularly good spot, and a dangerous one as traffic crested a hill at about 70 kilometres per hour (42 miles per hour for our American friends), and suddenly

arrived at an intersection.

I just finished setting up and testing the radar unit when the alarm went off and I got a reading of 114 kilometres per hour (for the Americans that's . . . uh . . . multiply by 1.6). I jumped onto the roadway and flagged the speeding car over to the curb. As I approached the driver's window, ready to rip the guy's head off for going so fast in the city, I noticed that the lady in the passenger seat was crying.

"Is there some emergency?" I asked with a smirk, recalling the speeder who had told me his brother was having a heart attack, and when I asked where this brother was, he said, 'in Hong Kong'.

The driver turned to me and spoke, "Her husband cut his finger off with a saw and we are rushing it to the hospital to have it sewn back on."

"Sure," I said, looking over at the passenger and raising my left eyebrow.

"Really, officer," the driver insisted, "and we don't have much time, it isn't wrapped in ice."

"And I suppose that's the finger in the young lady's lap" I said, still not believing what I was hearing.

The driver reached over and grabbed a cloth off the passenger's lap. He flipped it open and sure enough, there in the middle of the cloth, was a bloody finger.

"I knew that!" I said rather sternly, "Now get on your way to the hospital, but please slow down a bit." I thought I was going to woof my cookies.

* * *

I wanted to work the undercover stolen auto detail so bad I could taste it. The thought of setting up on bad guys and catching them in the act of stealing someone's car really turned my crank, and when I was finally accepted I was ecstatic. I hardly slept the day before my shift and was in the office an hour early to make sure I didn't miss a thing.

The team started to arrive, and we gathered in our little office to discuss the night's target and the plans for how we would be taking the guy down when he got into the stolen Camaro we had located. I could picture it now, watching from the dark as the perp skulked into the car, and then four of us racing to box him in before he could move. Yesss!

We finally hit the streets and I was all eyes. Everything that moved could be a stolen car and I wasn't going to let one get away from me. We turned onto a main road and there, right in front of us, was a drunk driver. I mean this idiot was all over the road. We didn't have time for a drunk, but he was not to be ignored. I grabbed the mike and called dispatch.

"Alpha 94, we have a 10-82 in front of us on Blank Street westbound. Can you get a blue and white over here to look after this guy before he kills someone?"

"10-4, Alpha 94," replied dispatch.

Moments later a blue and white pulled in behind the drunk and stopped him. We thanked the uniforms and drove on to more important things - catching guys in stolen cars.

It was about an hour later when the uniforms called us on the air.

"Is Alpha 94 on the air?"

"This is Alpha 94, go ahead."

"I just wanted to let you know that guy blew almost three times the legal limit."

"Great," I replied, "thanks for letting us know." I really wasn't interested.

"Oh, and by the way," continued the uniform, "did you guys run his plate before you called us?"

"No, why?" I asked, my level of interest taking a sudden turn.

"I didn't think so," came the voice over the speaker, "he was driving a stolen car!"

*   *   *

A Freudian slip occurs when the speaker means to say one thing and actually says something completely different, like the bandit in TALES FROM THE POLICE LOCKER ROOM who ran into the bank and yelled, "Put your stickin' hands in the air, this is a fuck up!" Or the TAC Team sergeant who meant to yell the command, "Spank the door!" but instead yelled out to his men, "Crank the whore!" These slips usually happen at the most inopportune time like the radio announcer who was describing the Academy Awards way back when and made the statement, "Marilyn Monroe is entering the theatre and all eyes are on her as she picks her seat."

This all brings me to an unnamed constable who went to a local coffee spot with his partner and decided to have a Coke instead of a coffee. The young waitress who served them was very well endowed and the officer found himself staring at her breasts while she was taking his order.

"Would you like a large Coke or a small one?" the server asked him.

"Oh, just a small one," he replied, finally looking her in the eyes, "I can't handle one of those big hooters."

*   *   *

I responded to a serious accident in which two cars had been struck by a semi coming from a packing plant. Several pigs had been

slaughtered at the packing plant and the semi was loaded to the hilt with guts. When the truck driver applied his brakes, the load shifted forward and the guts slopped out over the cab, covering both cars. The driver of one of the cars was knocked unconscious and was still in this state when I arrived on the scene. I was in the process of giving him a cursory examination to determine his injuries when he came to. He took one look at the guts all over his dashboard and started to scream.

I grabbed him by the shoulder and shook him hard. He was pulling the guts off the dashboard and trying to ram them into his shirt.

"They're not yours, they're not yours!" I was yelling at him. Now he started to scream and try to push them all back onto the dash.

"Whose are they?" he screamed at me.

"They belong to the pigs," I yelled, shaking him again.

"Oh, God," he screamed again, "I killed some cops."

By then the paramedics arrived and I left them to sort the mess out.

* * *

A pedestrian jay-walked right in front of our police car and my partner stopped him. We told him to get into the car, and we drove around the corner off the main drag so as not to block traffic while writing him the ticket.

As my partner began the summons I noticed that I was out of cigarettes. There was a 7-Eleven store across the street, so I jumped out of the car, ran across the street and bought some smokes. By the time I got back the pedestrian was gone and we continued our shift.

The next day when I arrived for work my sergeant called me into his office.

"Did you give some guy a jay-walking ticket last night?" he asked.

"John did." I said, "Why? Is there a problem?"

"Yeah, the guy complained that you did the same thing when you went to the 7-Eleven."

The nickel dropped. "Give me the ticket," I said, hanging my head.

He did.

*   *   *

Police officers have been known in the past, and probably will be into the future, for taking the odd peek at persons engaged in carnal manoeuvres and attempting to give them a bit of a fright by sneaking up and then flooding the car with flashlights.

We were working the outer limits of the

city one night and decided to take a run up to the local lovers lane and see if we could roust a few lovers. We drove up to the view point with our lights out and coasted the last few hundred metres into the parking lot with the engine off. There was only one car in the lot and the interior was in darkness. Ever so quietly, we slipped out of our cruiser with flashlights in hand. My partner waited while I crawled to the far side of the car, and then we both closed in simultaneously. At the exact same moment we jumped to our feet and flooded the interior of the car with light.

It was empty!

Then we heard a voice from the overhang of the hill right in front of the car. "Is everything all right, officers?"

We turned to see a young couple sitting on a blanket, overlooking the city, fully clothed, and just there for a talk.

"Everything's fine," I replied, beating a hasty retreat. "Just checking your vehicle to make sure it wasn't stolen."

There's no way on God's green earth he believed me!

*   *   *

Early in my police career I had what some would say was a very unusual officer coach. He had some different ways of handling complaints. During my training phase we attended what appeared to be a routine parking complaint. We went to a large apartment complex where the complainant occupied a unit on the second floor. Her complaint was that a large semi-trailer was parked directly outside of her balcony and had been running for quite some time. She could not sleep and the plates in her china cabinet were rattling all the time.

I went and opened the balcony door and the exhaust pipes common to tractor units were right at the height of her sliding doors. They were belching out noxious exhaust. It was impossible for her to open the door or she would have died of carbon monoxide poisoning. Prior to our arrival, she had canvassed other tenants, and no one seemed to know who the operator of the tractor unit was.

After listening to the entire complaint we excused ourselves and went outside.

"Well, rookie, what do we do now?" he asked in his best training voice.

"Tow it!" I said with glee.

"How?" he asked. "It's full!"

"Drive it away," I continued.

"And what happens when you run into something and damage the truck? Who's gonna pay for that?" he pressed.

"Well, what then?" I asked.

"Turn it off," he said with that look experienced officers give to rookies a lot.

I hopped into the cab and turned the ignition key to the off position. In seconds there was a beautiful silence.

We completed our shift and then went on three days off. When we came back and hit the streets again, our first call was to a "property damage". I recognized the address immediately.

We booked out at the scene to find a rather perturbed semi driver standing in the alley.

"What seems to be the problem, sir?" I asked in my best police voice.

"I came home for a few days with the family in the middle of a run and I took the wife and kids to the lake. When I came back some son-of-a-bitch had shut my tractor off! It's eighty degrees out here but it's over a hundred inside.

"What were you hauling?" I asked, showing genuine concern.

"Come and see," he insisted, walking to the rear of the truck and flinging the door open.

"A reefer with a full load of fish!" he yelled.

I almost gagged at the smell. My officer coach? He was the smart one, he stayed in the police car.

*   *   *

I never believed how easy it was to lose something as big as a car. I mean, we're talking three quarters of a ton of metal and plastic, usually painted in a bright colour. But still we lose sight of vehicles on a regular basis. However, this time was a little different.

I was on routine patrol in my assigned residential area when I heard the squeal of tires on pavement. This wasn't braking, it was acceleration. I became instantly more aware of my surroundings and scanned the street ahead for the obnoxious offender.

About a block ahead of me I saw a silver compact bounce over the curb of the 7-Eleven lot and drop onto the road with an unceremonious bang! As I watched, the vehicle skidded to its left and struck a parked car. The driver continued down the road without stopping. I couldn't believe I was witnessing a "smash and dash" and probably following a stolen car.

I accelerated hard and positioned my cruiser safely behind the fleeing car. I contacted dispatch and informed them of the incident. I also told them I was in pursuit.

The silver car was not slowing, even for the sharp "S" curve coming up. I had to back off. I was afraid I might cause the driver to crash, or worse yet, crash myself and get stuck with six hours of paperwork.

I briefly lost sight of the vehicle and I slid into the "S" curve with all the expertise I had learned at our high speed driving course. As I came out of the curve I arrived at a "T" intersection. I skidded to a stop and scanned the road, left - nothing; right - nothing! Where the hell did he go? He didn't have time to drive away, even at that speed!

I hated to lose a chase. I turned the car around and began retracing my steps. I informed dispatch that I had lost contact with the violator and was initiating an area search. Other cars began responding and joining me in the search for the bad guy.

I drove up and down the street about a dozen times and finally threw up my hands in defeat. I couldn't believe I had lost the car. I was just about to clear the scene and write the incident off when the dispatcher called me.

"Go ahead," I replied.

"If you attend at the blue house on the left hand side of the road about half way down the block, the owners have just come home and they have something for you."

I was sitting right in front of the house, so I turned to look - and there was the little silver car - embedded in the side of the blue house.

*   *   *

Bad guys really have a funny attitude sometimes. There are a number of guys I have arrested who just wanted to fight and there was no way around it. But some of them seem to have a certain code of rules or ethics.

We were patrolling a bar parking lot one sunny afternoon when we felt a bang on the side of our van. I hit the brakes and the bad guy was on me through the window. I forced the door open and we tumbled into the lot. I heard my partner exiting the vehicle and running to my assistance. This guy was wiry and hard to get into a control hold. My partner joined the fray and we continued to roll around on the pavement in the lot.

Something drew our attention and all three of us stopped fighting in mid-swing. We looked up to see the police van driving across the parking lot all by itself. I had forgotten to put the damn thing in park! I bolted to my feet and ran for the driver's door. To my amazement I was being followed by the bad guy - and my partner. We all reached the open door at the same time and I tried to jam the park brake on with my hand. The bad guy leaned in beside me and tried to push the brake pedal down with his hand, and my partner lunged over top of us to try and turn off the ignition.

Between the three of us we got the damn thing stopped only inches from a wall and a mountain of paperwork on the potential accident.

We took a short breather and then the bad guy said, "Where were we? Oh, yeah!"

With that he took a swing at me and the fight continued.

As long as I do this job I will never understand some people!

*   *   *

I always keep a pair of spit polished boots in my locker for going to court. I take pride in my appearance and I like to look my best in front of the judge. I went to my locker to get my shined shoes for court one day only to find that someone had gotten in and painted the words 'left' and 'right' on the toes with white-out. I didn't have time to clean them so I had to wear my scuffed work boots to court. My pride was a bit tinged but I would live.

When I returned from court I did a little investigation and found the culprit. I took the boots to him and we both had a good laugh. He agreed to clean them for me and reshine them. I left them with him and went about my duties.

The next day he brought me the boots with a spit shine that would make patent leather look dull. I thanked him very much, wrapped my prize in a terry cloth, and stored them gently in my locker once more.

A few days later I was to attend court again. I went to my locker, and to my relief my boots were still there, wrapped in the terry cloth and untouched. With pride I donned them and headed off to court. When my case was called I strode to the witness box with pride. To my amazement a chuckle rolled through the crowd behind me. I shrugged it off and gave my evidence.

When I returned to my locker after court, I removed the shiny boots and was engaged in rubbing a few scuff marks off the catwalks, when I noticed something white on the sole of the boot. I turned the boots over, and there printed in huge white letters on the sole of one boot was "HELP!", and on the other, "I'M GAY!" I should have known better!

* * *

We were dispatched to a call of unknown content one night. All we had was a call for assistance from some guy in an alley behind an address. I hated these kinds of calls. They could be a set-up for anything. But we had no choice, we had to attend.

My partner drove to the end of the alley and shut off the engine and lights. We allowed the car to roll into the alley in neutral so we would not attract too much attention. It was a hot summer night and the windows were down. Our senses were heightened for danger and we were expecting anything. Anything, that is, except what happened.

Without warning there were commando screams from both sides of the car, and something white and round exploded against our heads. We instinctively leaned inwards and banged our heads together as sloppy goo ran down our faces onto our uniforms. A second volley struck, this time the one on my side breaking against the door post and spraying the interior of the car. My partner ducked, and his projectile struck me on the right side of my head, exploding and covering me in goo.

"Get outta here!" I yelled as I drew my gun and tried to peer over the dashboard to locate our assailants. I couldn't see for the goo running into my eyes. I wiped it frantically.

My partner started the car and we fled the alley calling for backup. By now we began to realize we had been egged, and we were not amused. About four backup cars arrived and we closed the area down. My partner and I, covered from nape to navel in egg white and yolk, conducted the yard-to-yard search for the culprits.

We found them hiding in the third yard, called it in, and the backup rushed to the scene as we tackled the two. They were both males, about twenty-five years old, obviously of an age that should have known better than to egg a cop. We cuffed the two and were walking them down the alley to our police car when a late arriving backup unit pulled up behind us.

"Robbie? Dennis?" came the voice behind us. We turned with the bad guys and one of our colleagues got out of the car. "What the hell is going on?" he asked.

"These pricks just egged us," I replied. "Do you know them?"

"Well, sort of," he stammered. "They're my brothers visiting from out of town."

"Sorry, Paul," the one said. "We thought it was you who was gonna answer the call and we'd have some fun. Help us outta this will ya?"

He smiled and walked back to his car. "You got yourselves in, you get yourselves out."

He left.

We took the two 'not-so-happy' offenders into the station and gave them the third degree. We didn't charge them with anything but I don't think they'll ever try to set up their brother again.

*   *   *

Time for another swing at rookies.

Thanks rookies for giving me so much material!

I was still in the training stage with my mature and knowledgable officer coach, (yeah, right!) when it was time for us to conduct a walk-through at a local bar. It was ladies night and the place was jammed with women screaming their heads off as male dancers peeled their clothing off. I was a little taken aback by the crowd and stuck to my partner like glue. The two of us circled the women once, making sure that nothing untoward was taking place. I marvelled at the reaction of the women and flinched only slightly when someone in the crowd groped my butt.

We returned to the entrance and the coach said, "You wait here, I have to go take a whiz. I'll be right back."

I waited like a good little 'doo-bee', all the while not knowing I was being royally set up. The dancer finished his thing and the ladies screamed for more as he picked up his tips and clothing and left the stage. Suddenly the place went black as the lights went out and the announcer grabbed the mike.

"Ladies, we have a real special treat for you tonight! A volunteer has agreed to perform for your entertainment pleasure. Ladies, may I present to you, the hot, the muscular, the gyrating, gimme all you got, dancing patrolman!!!"

The lights exploded in colour and I was blinded as the spotlights flooded me at the doorway. The music blared and the screaming women turned towards me. My jaw dropped as they rushed me and I tried to turn and bolt out the door. Two of the biggest, strongest bouncers I have ever seen spun me around with a grin and shoved me towards the rushing crowd. In seconds I was surrounded by a mass of hollering, screaming women, who were groping and pulling and begging me to take it off. I couldn't believe my eyes. I dodged probing fingers and pulled stroking palms from my hair. Someone tried to kiss me and that created a second flood. I was squashed against the wall and was being lavished with kisses from everywhere. I could hardly breath. My tie disappeared, my hat went, I remember clasping my hands over my gun and my pepper spray which left me helpless. I couldn't fend them off now. They pressed me into the wall, and just as my name tag was yanked from my shirt, the announcer saved me by bringing on the next real dancer.

I was flabbergasted. I stood against the wall, trying to catch my breath, and taking stock of the missing pieces of my uniform. I was still dazed as my grinning partner plucked me from the bar and walked me towards the cruiser.

"Welcome to police work, son," he said with glee.

About three months later I completed my officer coach stage and was working day shift by myself. I was called to an elementary school and was to give the kids in a class a brief presentation on the police and let them play in the car for a while. I arrived at the school and was directed to the class where the teacher was waiting. I walked in calmly and the teacher stood.

"Well, isn't this nice!" she said loudly, " I remember you from the male strippers club. Are you still dancing part-time?"

I thought I was going to die!

CHAPTER EIGHT

I just can't resist taking a few more shots at the macho specialized members of the many police departments out there. They are highly specialized, heavily trained, and respond instantly to orders without question or hesitation. And if you believe that!!!

There is a lot of stress on those qualified positions and that's probably why they tend to goof off a little more seriously than the rest of us more sane types. While I was typing away on the last chapter of the manuscript I received a call from an anonymous police person who had a story to tell me about a certain police department's Armed Response Team. These are the guys who go into the serious weapons complaints and deal with potentially life and death situations. As a result they tend to be somewhat playful with each other between calls and the play can get a little rough. I relate the details in his words:

I'm a member of an Armed Response Team with a city police department. (Okay, that lets you Canadian Mounties and American FBI guys off the hook!) We need a lot of stress relief after some rather hair-raising calls and it tends to get a little dirty at times.

A few nights ago our team was out on a hot call and we had to take a guy down with a shot. It left us all a little tense and ripe for a practical joke. I went back to our debriefing room while the cleanup crew was still at the scene and I took out a pair of rubber gloves. I filled them to almost bursting with water and tied the ends with det-cord (a string which when rubbed or stretched causes a small controlled explosion with the force of a large firecracker). I got the ladder from the maintenance room and a few pieces of carpentry hardware for my joke. When I was finished I had tied the water-filled gloves to the end of a board and fastened the board to the ceiling with a hinge. I clipped the free end of the board to the ceiling and tied a string from the door knob to the clip. When the team returned whoever opened the door would get a good soaking.

I turned off the lights and hid behind

my locker. Soon the cars began to arrive and I could hear the team members talking in excited voices. They needed to come down from the adrenalin high of the call and I was going to help them do it with my joke.

I held my breath as I listened to someone fumbling with the door lock. I leaned around to watch as I heard someone say, "After you, sir."

My jaw dropped as I watched the chief step through the door and flip on the light. I bolted from the locker - too late! The string pulled the clip and released the board. The weight of the water-filled gloves caused the board to swing down on the hinge with great force and the conglomeration struck the chief with much more energy than I thought it would. As the gloves made contact with his face, the det-cord exploded, bursting the gloves, drenching him and my sergeant with water and blowing the chief's hat into the parking lot.

I held my breath, squeezed my eyes shut, and waited for my career to end instantaneously.

There was a long silence. A deathly silence. Finally it was broken with a chuckle, then a snort, then a healthy laugh, and finally a chorus of laughter.

When it all died down, the chief, who was mopping the water and det-chord char from his face and uniform said, "I had forgotten what it was like on the street and all the fun you guys have. Whoever did this, thanks. I feel like one of you again."

I breathed a sigh of relief, but I was not about to announce myself.

*   *   *

Things get even more rough. I always wanted to be a member of one of these elite groups, but having read these stories, I'm not so sure anymore. Let's continue.

Three times in a row! Three lousy times in a row they got me. The guys on my TAC Team started fastening det-cord to the door of my locker, and then to one of the hooks in the back of my locker, so when I opened the door it would blow up in my face and they would all laugh at me. Three bloody times in a row they got me. I was beginning to feel a little stupid. Of course, the fourth time I opened the door gently and peered inside, no cord, and I breathed a sigh of relief.

I finished dressing and the guys were ignoring me, which made me feel somewhat safe. Maybe they were going to start picking on someone else. I grabbed my gun belt from the hook on the back of the door and flung it around my waist as I usually do. Just as I clipped the buckle together there was a gawdawful explosion and the gun belt flew out of my hands. I stood there with det-cord residue all over my hands and my nice clean shirt. The buggers had put the cord on my belt buckle clip!

*   *   *

I had a great idea for a joke on one of the guys in my Armed Response Team. He had been playing jokes on the other guys for quite a while, and was smart enough that he had never been caught or been the recipient of a practical joke himself. In fact, if I must tell the truth, okay, the guy was my partner and that's how I knew he was playing these tricks on everybody.

We had a collection of fake drugs which we used when practicing our take-downs and searches. I snuck into the storage area one night and grabbed a huge bagful of phony cocaine and quietly returned to the locker room. I opened my partner's locker with one of the skills I had been taught on the team and took out his emergency call bag. Usually what is kept in there is all of the specialized gear we need to take with us on a hot call. I emptied the contents and lined the bottom of the bag with det-cord, then I stuffed the bag to bursting with the plastic bags of baking powder.

Just before I closed the zipper I attached the loose end of the det cord to it and slid it into place. I was careful to put the call bag back exactly as I had found it and to hide all of the normal contents where he wouldn't see them.

I contacted all of the other members of the team by pager and had them come to the office where we would be pretending to take a refresher class in combat techniques. My partner was the last one I contacted and the only one not to know that I had also set up a fake emergency call with our dispatcher.

We were all in the classroom and beginning a lecture when he arrived. He slipped in quietly and the instructor nodded to acknowledge him - also to let the rest of us know that he was here. We were all engrossed in the combat lecture when the instructor's pager went off. He excused himself, stepped into the hallway, and pulled his cell phone from his belt. He placed a call, and moments later ran back into the room as the loudspeaker on the wall announced, "Team A, we have a Code 1200 - red, corner of Smith Street and Jones Avenue. Shots are still being fired."

"We have a hot one," called out the instructor, grabbing his hat and heading for the locker room where the call bags were stored.

We all got up together and managed to let my partner be the first into the locker room. As he raced for his locker we hung back a little and made as if we were gathering weapons and stuff. He flung open his locker, grabbed the call bag, and tossed it to the floor. He bent over it to snap the zipper open and pull out the contents for the call, and we held our breath. As we watched he grabbed the zipper and opened it with a snap. I think he saw it just before the det cord went off. There was that split second of 'Oh, shit!' on his face just before the explosion. The det cord in the top of the bag tore open the bags of baking powder, and the cord in the bottom of the bag ejected the contents straight into his face. There he stood, looking just like Frosty the Snowman! Gotcha!!

*　　　　*　　　　*

Perry told me he needed just one more story about us macho specialty unit types so I decided to 'fess up' after he promised me immunity. So don't bother to ask him who gave him this story guys, and Perry, remember, I have the knowledge, I have the ability to deliver, and I will get even!

My partner and I had been at each other with practical jokes for about two months, and I guess our patience was actually starting to wear a little thin with each other. The jokes started off funny, but they had gotten a little

out of hand, and we were actually a tad pissed at each other for a few days. The last thing he had done to me was to sprinkle a little tear gas on my towel, and when I got out of the shower and used it, I was immediately overcome with stinging and burning and coughing and choking and sneezing and slobbering - if you get the picture. That's when I decided to call a truce. Enough was enough. We agreed and got back to the business of being partners.

But you have to know that I just couldn't let him get one up on me! I was patient - oh so patient. I waited an entire month and then I just couldn't hold it inside anymore. While he was in the shower I sprayed tear gas on his stick deodorant and put it back in his open locker. Out he came, dried himself off, and immediately slapped the deodorant on. In about six seconds he began to dance and yelp and flap his arms like the "I feel like chicken tonight" commercial. As he realized what I had done, he raced back to the shower and flooded his armpits with cool water.

While he was wetting down, I was apologizing and laughing and assuring him that the truce was back on.

"I guess you owed me one or two, you prick," he chuckled as he dried off again and took his shaving gear to the sink. He quickly shaved and was telling me about the work he had been doing on his basement at home as he slapped on the aftershave. I stood back. His face dropped and he let out a yell, "You son-of-a-bitch! In my aftershave!"

Back into the shower he fled for the third time and nearly drowned himself trying to get that shit off his face. I was in stitches.

As he turned off the water, I passed him his towel and he took it. He was just about to open it and dry himself off again when the thought struck him. "Sure, you little asshole, and now you've covered my towel with the shit. You think I'm that stupid? I took your towel home and cleaned it, I know it's safe, gimme the damned thing!"

I went to my locker and retrieved the towel which he had brought to me after dousing it with tear gas last month and which he had told me he would clean for me. I passed him the towel and grinned. "Okay, you win, I guess it was stupid to try and get you three times in a row."

"Damned right," he said as he buried his face in my towel. It took about four or five seconds. "You bastard," he yelled between coughs and gags and sputters. He staggered back into the shower for the fourth time and I made a b-line for the door.

Ma - cho,   ma - cho   Man!

Let's hit the streets with the crews again and look into a few more of those stories of bravado, machismo, pepperoni and green peppers. Hey, we don't always do doughnuts!

*   *   *

One of our deputy chiefs was up acting as chief while the big cheese was away on summer holidays. He was the kind of guy who caused havoc every time he opened his mouth, and we were used to his sometimes-not-so-clever edicts that emanated from his office at times. While he was acting chief, we had three incidents in which our K-9 units bagged bad guys, and they all got themselves bit. The deputy was taking a bit of flack from the media and he tried to explain that we worked our dogs naked. What that really means is that they do not wear a collar or a leash when tracking. But when our astute deputy said it, he made it sound like the handlers were naked. The question was immediately asked by one of the female reporters,

"Isn't that a little dangerous when working in heavily thicketed areas?"

The deputy did his best to back peddle but he didn't recover much on the 11:00 o'clock news that night. He did manage to make an immediate, well thought out and decisive statement though.

"I guess, in order to avoid afflicting too much trauma on the arrestees, we will instruct all of our K-9 handlers to work their dogs on line. At no time will a dog be loose when in pursuit of a suspect and in that manner we can eliminate further biting."

We were immediately instructed to use our fifty foot leashes when tracking suspects and informed that the next handler who allowed his dog to bite when off line would be in serious kah-kah.

My very next call was a break and enter at a department store in the downtown area. When I arrived, the street guys had the building contained and were waiting for me to go through the area with my dog. They believed the bad guy to still be inside, and the air crackled with tension as I snapped the fifty foot leash onto my dog. Obviously the bad guy was still there because the dog took off like a shot, right through the broken door and down the lingerie aisle. It was all I could do to keep up with him on the end of the leash, and I did not want to be the first guy disciplined for letting him bite. I bounded along behind him, my feet touching the floor about every six feet, and being flung around the corners like a skater on a crack the whip chain. He raced past the sporting goods and into the electronics section and started to growl and bark as we rounded the corner into the household department.

Suddenly the bad guy bolted from his cover and began running towards the exit. My dog leaped and I barely managed to hold him back from taking a piece of the guy's ass. But the bad guy got himself cornered in housewares and jumped a counter into the cooking and tableware section. We followed like a buzz saw looking for a log to shred and took up the chase again. The leash was stretched to its limits as I tried desperately to keep up. We fled down an aisle and began passing a centre aisle display of Royal Doulton china, which was on special that week. Just as we reached the far end of the display and I was breathing a sigh of relief, the bad guy doubled back down the opposite side of the china display. I had no time to react as my dog turned the corner and followed. My jaw dropped as the leash went tight across the bottom of the display and the china began to tumble. There was an ungodly sound of shattering, expensive dishes and figurines which seemed to go on forever as the leash worked its way under the dis-

play. By the time I managed to pull in a few feet of leash, the entire display was down and I could hear the bad guy yelling, "Get this damned dog off me! OW!! He's biting me! Get him off!"

When the department store owners showed up, the first thing they asked was, "Whose idiotic idea was it to use a dog on a leash in a department store?"

For the rest of our chief's holidays we barely saw or heard from the deputy. When the chief returned, there was a small eruption in his office at the executive meeting, and the deputy chief was rumoured to have slinked away licking his wounds. O' the dogs, we run them naked again.

*   *   *

I had just purchased a brand new Honda Goldwing and I was as proud as a kid with a new puppy. I went to the dealership on my day off and picked up my new toy. Ripples of excitement ran through me as I swung my leg over the rear fender and settled down onto the soft leather of the saddle. I would be in my glory riding back and forth to the police station on this baby.

I turned the key on and pressed the starter. The low thrum of the engine caused my blood to race a little faster and I was ready to roll! I pulled out onto the main street, twisted the accelerator, and slipped ever so smoothly into the flow of traffic. I was cool!

I hadn't ridden ten blocks when I saw a dirtbag on a Harley warping his way through traffic behind me. He cut in and out like a bee darting from plant to plant, and as he blew past me I saw him take a second to look at my new bike and sneer. A sea of brake lights appeared in front of me as he incessantly changed lanes without signalling and cut off other motorists trying to use the road. He finally had to stop for a red light, first in line of course, and I glided quietly up beside him on my Honda. I didn't identify myself as a police officer but did get his attention and said, "You know, you're going to kill someone riding like that in traffic. Why don't you give a little consideration to the other drivers?"

The biker scowled at me and replied, "Why don't you piss off and get a Harley!" With yet another sneer he accelerated away through the red light, nearly causing a crash as he did. I made a mental note of his licence plate number.

The following day I was on shift and drove my new Honda to work where I was assigned to the Traffic Division. I selected the newest and shiniest Harley police bike from the fleet and booked it out for the day. I drove straight to the dirtbag's house, parked the bike right beside his, and strode to the door. After a severe knocking I managed to rouse him from bed (at 8:30 A.M.) and he came to the door.

"What the hell do you want?" were his first words to me.

I smiled and removed my motorcycle helmet.

"Do you remember yesterday, telling a guy on a Honda to 'piss off and get a Harley'?"

"Yeah," the biker laughed.

"Well, I have a Harley now, so let's see your registration, insurance and driver's license, pal."

* * *

DUMB CRIMINAL ALERT!!!

Apparently a shoplifter took exception to the fact that store security was arresting him and he bopped one of the arrestors in the nose. This of course resulted in a foot chase. The bad guy fled the store with the two security persons in hot pursuit. The shoplifter was as determined to escape as security was to apprehend him, and the chase became quite wild as they darted through traffic, fell over the hoods of vehicles and slammed into pedestrians on the sidewalk.

I was just beginning my shift and had an armload with my briefcase, radar, shotgun and rain gear because of the clouds in the west. I made my way into the locked compound and was walking towards my police car when I heard the commotion. I looked and saw a guy running down the back alley, being pursued by two others. There was no gate on the back of the compound, so I was not in a position to assist in the chase. As I watched, the bad guy made a sudden veer to the left, grabbed the chain link in the fence and began to climb it. I dropped my equipment and went to stand between the two police vans where he would come down. As he dropped from the top of the eight foot fence I reached out and grabbed him by the scruff of the neck. I pushed his face into the wire fence and slipped his arm up behind him in an arrest hold.

"You're under arrest for . . ." I didn't know what the hell he had done.

Just then the two pursuees arrived, out of breath and sweating profusely. They leaned up against the fence, wheezing and holding the wires for support. I looked at one of them and then nodded towards my arrest. The security guy managed to wheeze out "shhhhhoplllllifterrr!"

". . . shoplifting," I said, barely missing a beat.

I love it when the bad guy comes right to you!!

*   *   *

I have mentioned before that rookies are like raw meat, but this is one of the best rookie stories I have ever heard.

I was such a new rookie that when people asked me how long I had been a policeman I still looked at my watch instead of my calender. At the beginning of each shift we meet, just like the guys on Hill Street Blues, and discuss any problem areas, special arrests, major criminals, etc. I listened intently as the sergeant read off a complaint about a gay man who was trying to pick up men and young boys in the washroom of a local department store. To date, the victims had been so shaken, they were unable to provide a description of the bad guy, but his pattern of M.O. determined that he would make an attempt sometime this afternoon.

The sergeant looked right at me. "Johnson," he said tersely, "you're the newest member in the area and this guy won't recognize you. Slip into your civvy clothes, you're going on undercover today."

I was thrilled. How many members of my graduating class would be chosen for undercover work with only a few days on the street? I would be able to brag about this at our first class reunion!

I changed back into my civilian clothes

222

and went to the sergeant for instructions. He gave me the address and told me to pay attention to everyone who used the washroom while not drawing attention to myself. When the bad guy showed up and made an advance on me, I was to arrest him and call for backup.

Boy, if my classmates could see me now! I drove my unmarked police car to the department store, checked my gun in my shoulder holster, pulled my jacket a little tighter to make sure it was covered and stepped out of the car, feeling not unlike Hunter. In a few moments I was in the washroom in question and made myself busy by washing my hands as people came in and out. In about half an hour I realized that this was a very busy washroom and my hands were beginning to wrinkle badly as I continued to wash them.

I decided on a new form of cover and I went to the urinal. I unzipped my fly and pulled my penis out to add to the reality of the stakeout. There I stood.

I stood with my dink in my hand for four hours, and even got desperate enough that I started winking at guys who used the urinal beside me to see if I could flush out the bad guy. I was into the frustrating fifth hour of my first stakeout when I suddenly realized I had been had. There was no bad guy and there would be no bragging at my class reunion.

*   *   *

It was the Winter Olympics. This was going to be the most exciting event in the history of our police department. We all had special duties to perform and had been practicing for months. Finally it was here! This was the night before the games and excitement was heavy in the air. My assignment for this shift was to walk the stadium where the opening ceremonies would be held the following morning. My partner and I had divided the stadium in two and we each walked half in a figure eight, meeting every thirty minutes at centre field where we would exchange information, jokes and the like.

The assignment quickly became boring, and in order to lighten the load a bit we would play jokes on each other as we passed in centre field. It started off with simple things like kicking the other guy's foot as he passed and making him trip, then running before he could retaliate. We were having our own Practical Joke Olympics, right where the opening ceremonies would take place. He took my hat once and I threw a bucket of sawdust at him, making him think it was water, and so it went.

At about 4:00 A.M. we met in the middle of the field and my partner lit a cigarette. We stopped to talk and rest our legs a bit and soon began discussing the events of the day to come. We agreed that the police should have had an entry into the torch parade, and decided that we could have been it and how much fun it would have been to be seen on international TV.

"Yeah, just like this!" I said, jumping up and grabbing my partner in a dance hold. Together we strutted the tango around centre field, cheek to cheek, laughing and even getting in a few dips. At about 6:30 A.M. our relief arrived and it was time for us to go home.

"Boys, boys, boys," they were saying as they met us centre field.

"What?" I asked, very tired from all the walking.

"Bad enough you two had to stop for a smoke at centre field, but the tango thing!"

"How the hell do you know about that, was somebody watching us?" I asked.

"Only half the world," he replied. "The TV guys were doing a night before special and part of it included showing the calm and deserted stadium, awaiting the arrival of the torch. There were the two of you doing your torch dance, dipping and twirling cheek to cheek in front of millions!"

* * *

I stopped a guy for drunk driving one

night, and to my amazement when I got him into the police car I discovered that he was Italian and didn't speak a word of English. I needed an interpreter, but where the hell was I going to find one at 3:00 A.M.? A flash of brilliance! There was an all-night pizza place about half way to the station and I could stop there. The cook was Italian and he would be able to translate for me.

I pulled into the parking lot of the pizza place and motioned for the owner to come out to the car. I told him of my situation and he was happy to go and get the cook for me. Soon the cook arrived, covered in flour, and smelling much like a number three special. He slipped into the car beside me and asked me in a heavy accent what I wanted him to do.

"Ask this guy what his name is, for starters, " I said, pen poised over paper.

With that the cook turned to my arrest and said in a loud voice, "Hey, whatza you name?"

* * *

When I was assigned to K-9 I loved doing building searches. There was the ever present tension of possibly finding a bad guy and searching a building in the dark. It always gave me a rush.

One night I was dispatched to a leather

clothing store which had been broken into, and when I arrived, the street guys had the place contained. They didn't know if the bad guy was still inside or not, but the whole front door had been smashed in. My adrenalin began to pump as I called my dog from the back of the car, and we stepped to the broken door. I shone my flashlight down the aisle and we climbed in, and immediately lit up a tall wooden Indian figure against the far wall. My dog took off on a dead run and came to an abrupt stop, sniffing the wooden Indian and giving a quiet "woof" of disgust.

I was standing with my back to the door and all of the police unit lights were behind me. Suddenly my dog turned and glared at me. He lowered his head, snarled and bolted down the aisle towards me.

"Jesus," I thought, he can only see my silhouette and he thinks I'm the bad guy. His lips were drawn back over his ears and he had that 'I'm going to bite you!' look in his eyes. I had nowhere to go and I began yelling at him frantically.

Just as he leapt in the air he turned a little to my right and landed squarely on top of a full length wolf coat on the counter top. I stared in disbelief as he grabbed a mouthful of fur, tore it from the coat, spit it out and lunged at the material again.

"Good God, stop!" I yelled. "This'll cost

me a month's salary you stupid son-of-a-bitch!"

"All right, all right, I won't fight anymore and I'll pay for the coat myself," came a terrified voice from under the material.

I grasped the collar of the ripped and torn fur and flung it back. There was the bad guy huddling under the coat as the dog tore its way through to him.

*   *   *

You military police types - bet you thought you were going to get away scott free didn't you. Not!

The summer of 1956 had been particularly hot, and most of the families on the military base had taken to sleeping with their windows open to catch whatever slight breeze would cross their beds. The homes were wartime and they were built with the old style removable storm windows for winter. Each window had a small sliding screen which fit into the sill when you raised the inside sash in the summer, and these were in full use throughout the married quarters of the army camp.

Many families had taken to sleeping in the nude and on top of the sheets as the humidity and heat were stifling. Unfortunately, an enlisted pervert had discovered this and he took to skulking around bedroom windows at night, getting his jollies by viewing naked women sleeping or in various states of undress as they prepared for bed.

One night, the hapless voyeur displayed a little too much enthusiasm during climax and managed to draw the attention of the captain's wife, whom he had been watching undress. She screamed, he jumped from the porch roof, and the captain came running upstairs to see what the hell was going on. Mrs. Captain filled him in on the heinous offence and the next day the alert was raised on the base. Over the next ten days, the voyeur was spotted numerous times, but could never be caught. He always managed to make good his escape and the wives in the camp were becoming very concerned.

A plan was devised by the military police. Each man would be issued a radio which would remain on throughout the night. If anyone saw the voyeur, they would raise the alarm and the area could be flooded with MP's in an instant. A great plan!

The following night an MP sergeant's wife was sleeping nude on top of the sheets when she heard something on the roof outside her window. Rather than screaming, she nudged her husband who was already awake, and he slid quietly off the bed. His commando training kicked in and he slithered on his belly across the hardwood floor towards the window. He raised onto his hands and knees and looked through the screen from an angle behind the curtains, and there was the pervert with his face pressed tightly against the mesh.

In a single movement he swung his fist and made contact with the voyeur's jaw, and with the other hand called his MP squad to alert on the radio. The pervert fell from the roof with a solid thud and was running before he hit the ground. In seconds the area was filled with eleven MP's, all running with radios in hand, yelling instructions to each other, holding flashlights, and every one of them buck naked.

Lights came on in homes around the area and doors began to fly open. Women came to the doors and then screamed as naked MP's flew past them, heels clapping and balls flapping in the night air. Suddenly the chaos was broken with the sound of the sergeant's voice over the radio.

"All members will immediately return to their homes and don clothing before continuing the search."

Everyone complied, and while they were doing so, the pervert slipped from his cover behind some bushes and disappeared into the night.

The following morning the sergeant received a call from the medical clinic and was asked to attend. He did so, and when he met with the doctor, he was presented with a large piece of mesh from a screen window.

"Do you recognize this?" the doctor asked.

"I think it's a hunk of my screen from last night. Where the hell did you find it?"

"Embedded in this guy's face," he said as he pulled back the curtain to reveal the pervert, handcuffed to the bed and sporting a huge black eye complete with cuts.

CHAPTER NINE

The Charter of Criminal's Rights, as it has become known in Canada, continues to be a sore spot with most police officers. Until the Charter was changed, it was enough to inform a criminal that he was under arrest for whatever offence he had committed, and then to tell him that he had the right to contact a lawyer. Police officers have known forever that most criminals are not brain surgeons, but they can understand the basics: a) you did something bad; b) I caught you and arrested you; c) you can call your lawyer. I don't know about you but I don't think this is too difficult even for limited intelligence to grasp.

Enter the lawyers.

As a result of the meticulous meddling provided by lawyers we must now tell the bad guy the following:

a) You are under arrest for_____(this part hasn't changed much, and I agree that if someone is arrested, it is probably a good thing to let them know for what).

b) Before we proceed with our investigation we are obliged to inform you that:

  i) You don't have to talk to us;

  ii) Anything you do say can be written down and used in evidence against you;

  iii) You have the right to contact your lawyer;

  iv) We will provide you with a telephone and a telephone book to assist you in locating your lawyer;

  v) If you do not have a lawyer we will provide you with a list of legal aid lawyers which you may contact free of charge;

  vi) We will provide you with a telephone and telephone numbers of the legal aid lawyers in this area.

  vii) Do you understand all of this and would you like to contact a lawyer before we continue?

I don't know about you, but if I was a bad guy and the cops told me this, do you really think I would tell them anything? This charter has been changed probably a dozen times in the past ten years to the point where the Canadian police officer has no idea which charter was read to which accused on which date.

I have a solution. Ah! You say, we were sure you would! Well, you're right. The following is a final draft of a proposed change to the Charter of Rights which should cover all the bases and not require future overhauling:

RIGHT TO COUNSEL

I am arresting you for_____ (insert appropriate criminal charge here).

It is my duty to inform you that you have the right to retain and instruct counsel without delay. You have the right to telephone any lawyer you wish, even if he is vacationing in the Bahamas or some other exotic location. The taxpayers will pay for the long distance bill. It is my duty to ask you if you are feeling depressed about your current arrest. 1-800-555-1234 is a toll free number that will put you in touch with a Legal Aid psychologist free of charge. You also have the right to advice from a Legal Aid lawyer free of charge. It is further my duty to ask if all is well with your family and pets at home. 1-800-555-1235 is a toll free number that will put you in touch with a Legal Aid veterinarian for free advice in relation to the health of your pets. Also, how is your car running? I have a list of reasonably priced mechanics who will inspect your vehicle at this time. Are you hungry? If so, I will buy you something to eat because your welfare is my highest priority. 1-800-555-1236 is a toll free number that will put you in touch with a Legal Aid duty counsellor for free advice on these rights. Do you understand? Do you wish to call a lawyer, psychologist, veterinarian or mechanic now? Do you wish to drive the police cruiser to the police station?

I think that ought to cover it, don't you?

* * *

And now for something completely different.

A local radio crew started reading off lists on the air called "The Ten Things (in whatever kind of sport or work) That Sound Nasty ... but Aren't!"

I forwarded to them the following list which was read on air:

Here is the list of the top ten things in police work that sound nasty . . . but aren't:

10) A surreptitious entry;

9) An inside job;

8) Crack house;

7) The guy was butt stroked;

6) Here come the Dicks;

5) I skinned her when I cuffed her;

4) And then, Your Honour, I struck him with my eighteen inchstick!

3) May I see your particulars;

2) Up against the wall.

And the number one thing in police work that sounds nasty but isn't:

1) Spread 'em.

All right already, let's get back to my buds n' budettes in blue!

*   *   *

In the past our guys used to make good use of their flashlights when subduing a person who was a danger to others. We would use the flashlight like a nightstick and the result was usually effective. Our management decided that it was not proper for police officers to go around striking bad guys with flashlights (cause they might get sued) and so decided to purchase twenty-eight inch batons and instruct the entire department in their proper use.

The batons were issued and training commenced. It was rather intense and the program lasted a full three days. By the time I completed the instruction I felt ready to confront someone with the baton if the issue arose. I had perfected such moves as three-from-the-ring, upper-cradle, lower-cradle, and the ever popular standing-modified. I was ready!

My next shift was a late afternoon, and after putting on my uniform I slid the baton from my locker, and thrilled to the sound of ebony on steel as I slid the instrument into the carrying ring on my equipment belt. Look out, bad guys, I have a new tool and I am fully trained in its use! I stepped in front of the locker room mirror, placed my hand on the butt of the baton, and marvelled at my cat-like prowess as I walked through all of the martial arts style moves I had learned. With satisfaction I slipped the baton back into its ring, hiked up my equipment belt, and headed for the street.

My beat that evening took me through an area where the local drug dealers stood on the corner and sold their wares. I spotted an unsavoury character on a corner and approached him to conduct some intelligence gathering. As I walked towards him he bolted and ran. I took up the chase and was closing the distance quickly, baton rattling noisily against my metal flashlight with each stride. I caught up to him in about a block and with

out warning he spun and attacked me. I reacted with all the training my department had instilled in me for the past three days. I took the proper stance, threw my hand up in the air to distract the attacker as I had been taught, reached for the baton . . . and promptly drew my flashlight and struck the suspect. Oh well, guess it'll take a little time to break old habits.

*　　　*　　　*

The call was a break and enter. It was my job to attend the scene and gather forensic evidence such as fingerprints and photographs. I rang the doorbell and was let in by a young lady. I introduced myself and my jaw dropped as I viewed the state of the living room. It looked like a tornado had just passed through it. The cushions were off the couch, the coffee table was on its side, there were papers and clothing tossed all over the room. It was a disaster area! I never could understand why bad guys had to trash a house after they had broken in. It made no sense. I felt badly for the lady and tried to console her.

"Boy," I said, "did they make a mess in here! You're going to have a tough time cleaning up this trash job."

The young lady looked at me and raised her eyebrows.

"They weren't in this part of the house," was all she said.

*　　　*　　　*

"I did it! I did it!" the guy was yelling as we approached him.

"Did what?" I asked as I came to stand over the man who was trussed up like Nell in the Dudley Do-Right cartoons.

He was tied from head to foot in rope and laying on a railway track with his head on one rail and his knees on the other.

"The hit and run, the hit and run. I did it! Just get me off here before the damn train comes. I'll pay for the damage and I'll take the charges, just get me the hell off here!"

"What are you talking about?" I asked the man as my partner and I lifted him from the tracks and began untying him.

"I ran into my neighbour's brand new truck last night when I came home from the bar, and I hid my car so he wouldn't know, but he saw me and he and his buddies grabbed me tonight and tied me up and stuck me here on the Goddamn train tracks, and I don't wanna die, so get me off here! I did it, I did it!"

"Calm down, buddy," I said with a chuckle as I removed turn after turn of the yellow nylon rope. "This is a closed siding that hasn't had a train on it in twenty years. You've been had and now you've been busted."

*   *   *

We were involved in a pursuit which began in the city and ran out into the country. Our dispatch called ahead to the Mounties and they set up a roadblock with a spike belt to deflate the tires of the bad guy. We had two marked police cars in the chase and a K-9 car following in case the bad guy dumped the car and went on foot.

We entered the outer limits of a small town and saw the overhead lights of the Mountie car flashing in the distance. Aha! We had him now. All we had to do was guide him over the spike belt and his tires would deflate in a few hundred yards and he would be ours.

As the fleeing car approached the road-block he suddenly dropped off the pavement and cut the corner across a ditch and lawn. Not wanting to do further damage to the lawn, we manoeuvred our police car between the roadblock and the curb. The backup car and the K-9 followed us in hot pursuit. We accelerated out of the corner and suddenly the car became sluggish and wouldn't steer properly. It became embarrassingly obvious that we had driven over the damned spike belt while the bad guy had missed it. I decided to pull over and let the other cars pass me, but as I did, I noticed that they too were pulling over. In a flash the Mountie car passed us all and we heard moments later that he had the vehicle stopped and one in custody. There we sat, sheepish as hell.

A few weeks passed and we were alerted that the Mounties were pursuing a stolen vehicle towards the city. We quickly set up a roadblock with a spike belt between the two police vehicles and waited. We heard the wailing of the Mountie's siren in the distance approaching fast, and it wasn't long before we could hear the roar of racing engines.

In a flash both vehicles leapt over the horizon and were on us. The bad guy had no choice and was successfully funnelled onto the spike belt. We were about to remove a police car to allow the Mountie through when he followed the bad guy across the spike belt. Both vehicles travelled the standard few hundred yards and came to rest on flat tires. The Mountie bolted from his car and caught his man. After he had the guy in cuffs and in the back of his car he walked over to us.

"Mounties three, City Police one," he said, pointing to the disabled police cruiser.

"Oops!" said my partner.

*   *   *

A lady reported that her apartment had been broken into, and the investigating officers requested that I attend to fingerprint the place in hopes of getting a hit. The apartment was very different in that the upper bedroom was designed like a barn loft and actually had a ladder going up to it instead of a staircase.

The lady of the house was rather attractive and made no bones about being single as we examined various rooms in the apartment. I was not having any luck finding something which gave a suitable surface for fingerprinting. She suggested we try the bedroom and bolted up the ladder ahead of me. I followed, brush and print powder in hand, and popped my head up over the end of the ladder. My eyes were at floor level and I was nose to nose with a vibrator.

"Nothing here to print" I said, readying for a hasty retreat.

The woman grabbed the vibrator and thrust it at me.

"Here, you can print this," she said.

"I don't think so," I replied, slinking back down the ladder.

*　　　　*　　　　*

My dog and I were out doing a track on a couple of dirtbags who had broken into a shop and been scared off by the alarm. We knew they had run away on foot and we were on a good trail which led down into a ravine behind the business. When we reached the bottom of the hill the track seemed to just disappear and my doggie couldn't pick it up anywhere. While he was trying to locate the track I decided there was time enough to empty my bladder against a nearby tree in the darkness. I strode up to a huge cottonwood tree and unzipped my fly. My dog must have taken the hint because he joined me at the side of the tree. There we both were merrily watering the foliage when the police helicopter arrived on scene and hovered directly above us. The observers turned on the night sun floodlight and it became like daylight. I winced as the light momentarily blinded me. I caught a brief movement out of the corner of my eye, and suddenly realized my dog was peeing on the stolen property which had been dumped there by the bad guys. I was peeing on the bad guys!

*　　*　　*

Part of our job with the Identification Section is to attend fatal traffic accidents and photograph the scene for court purposes. I was doing just that one night when a drunk wandered into the middle of the accident location and began kicking debris around. The placement of nearly every piece of evidence can be crucial and it was necessary to explain to this guy that it was not good for him to be moving the pieces.

I took him by the arm and directed him to the side of the road.

"Look," I said, "we can't have you rummaging around in the middle of an accident scene, so why don't you just move on."

He didn't reply. He just stood there swaying back and forth, looking at me with half closed eyes. I hoped he wouldn't stagger back into the scene and puke on the evidence. Leaving him there, I went back to my camera, and was just ready to take a shot when I saw the drunk stagger into the picture frame and wave at me. That was enough!

This time I grabbed him and took him sternly to the curb.

"Stay outta my damn way," I yelled at him.

"Grrpphmmmmnphh," was the reply, accentuated with a fist to the side of my head.

The fight was on. For a drunk, he was pretty accurate and he managed to land a few good punches on my face. We were rolling towards my camera when I saw the traffic sergeant running to my aid. He grabbed the drunk and hauled him to his feet. As he attempted to twist the guy's arm behind him, the drunk spun and punched him in the chest. I managed to scramble to my feet and launched a vicious kick towards the guy's stomach. At about the same time the sergeant was throwing a punch to the drunk's midsection and we connected with each other. I caught him square in the knuckles with the toe of my boot and the sergeant let go his grip. About that time the drunk passed out. By then, other officers were coming to our rescue, and there was the sergeant dancing around holding his knuckles.

The drunk went to the tank, I went back to my camera, and the sergeant - well, he went to the hospital with two broken knuckles.

*   *   *

I'm a police woman and my partner always liked to go to calls with the lights and siren going whenever possible. I think it's one of those male-toy things that some men officers suffer from. We were dispatched to a drunk on a street corner in rush hour. Someone was worried he might stagger into traffic and get himself killed. As we arrived on the scene my partner switched on the overhead lights. We couldn't miss our drunk, he was the one doing ballet dancing on the corner and singing some indiscernible tune.

I walked up to the guy and suggested he should come with us for the sake of his own safety. He grinned at me and winked, saying,

"Honey, I'll go anywhere with you."

I took him by the arm and directed him back to the police car. When I got to the door I discovered my partner had locked us out. I waited while he went into a store to get a coat hanger. Bad enough we were locked out of the car in rush hour, but the overheads were on and attracting looks like ET.

During the unlocking ceremonies the drunk decided to get a little affectionate. While I was engaged in helping my partner, the drunk reached out and grabbed my butt. I dropped the coat hanger, spun him around, slapped the cuffs on him and bent him over the trunk of the car. "Stay there!" I said sternly.

We finally got the car open, and were on our way to the tank with our scoop, when we saw a guy take a face plant on the sidewalk next to us. He went down hard and we called it in. I bounded from the car and checked on the guy. He was having a heart attack and I started CPR on him. My partner called for an ambulance and we worked on the guy until the paramedics arrived. They coded him after checking his vital signs and we stopped our CPR. We had to wait on scene until the body removal people showed up, and then we assisted them in wrapping the corpse, placing it onto the stretcher and sliding it into the back of the black body van.

We got back into the police car and had

almost forgotten about our drunk when he piped up from the back seat.

"Listen," he said, a little more sober than before. "I'll behave myself, just don't kill me like you did that fella, okay?"

*   *   *

My partner should have been in Traffic. He loved to write tickets and took every opportunity to uphold the law of the road and issue what he called 'driver training aids' to errant motorists.

We pulled over a car for making an unsafe lane change, and during the course of the investigation he discovered that the driver did not have his license with him, nor did he have his registration papers for the car. I watched as my partner wrote up three tickets for the driver. He exited the police van and took all of the tickets with him. After having served copies on the accused, he returned to the van and reached in through the driver's side window, placing the remaining copies of the tickets on the dashboard. About the same time I began to feel a bit warm from the sun beating through my window, so I rolled it down to get some fresh air. A gust of wind blew through the van and plucked the top ticket off the dashboard like a feather.

My partner saw it float past him and

ran after it. Just as he reached for the ticket the wind blew again and it fluttered away from him. It was like something from an old time movie. I mean every time he reached for it, the wind blew it away. By the third time I was in tears with laughter and I noticed the driver of the offending vehicle beginning to chuckle. My partner made a frantic grab for the ticket just before it blew onto a main thoroughfare filled with rush hour motorists. Suddenly there he was, standing straight and tall, hands out in both directions stopping traffic. When all the cars had stopped he again began chasing the ticket across the street. It finally got caught in the gutter on the far side and he retrieved it. Now that's a true Traffic Man!

* * *

That last story reminded me of a confession I must make at this time. Yup, it's me. I was working warrant detail one summer evening and I had a stack of traffic warrants as thick as the Bible. I had a police van and was making the rounds to pick up as many people as I could before heading downtown to get the tickets paid. I ended up with eight in the cage in the back, one in the passenger seat, and four in the rear seat of the van. I was driving towards the downtown core on a main street when the lady beside me rolled down her window. You guessed it! The wind blew in and picked up all seventy-five warrants. In a flash they were spread all over the road.

I flipped on the overhead lights and darted from the van. In seconds I knew it was hopeless by myself. I returned to the van and asked how many would like to work off their fines. Every one said yes, so I opened the cage and the side doors and everyone hopped out to help. While I stopped traffic, they scampered all over the place retrieving their warrants.

When we arrived at the back counter I asked to see the Justice of the Peace on duty and explained to him what had happened. I told him they had all agreed to help me retrieve the warrants and had saved the city a lot of time and effort in doing so. He agreed and ordered all thirteen before him at once.

"This officer tells me that you assisted him in a time of dire emergency. Is this true?" he asked.

"Yes," they replied together.

"In light of your acts of kindness I vacate the warrants for all of you, make a finding of not guilty on those of you who have not yet gone to trial, and commute the outstanding fines to 'time in custody'.

They were happy, the JP was happy, I was happy, cool!

*   *   *

Here was the plan. A guy had called saying he was going to commit suicide with a handgun and two car crews were assigned to the call. This guy lived in an apartment, and when we arrived at the building, I met with the manager and got a key from him. We went to the door of the apartment, and this was what was supposed to happen. On our signal, our dispatcher would phone the bad guy and tell him we were outside. I would unlock the door quietly, and as he came to look out the peephole, I would open the door quickly and knock him to the floor. I would then step in and move quickly to the left, allowing the other two officers to aim their pepper spray foggers at him and incapacitate him with the spray. Simple, but effective.

We arrived at the door and I slid the key into the lock. I twisted it silently and signalled that the door was now unlocked. One of the other guys informed dispatch that we were ready and she made the call. In a few seconds the bad guy came to the door and peered out through the peephole just as we figured he would. I put my shoulder into the door and struck him squarely on the chest. As planned, I ran into the apartment and made a quick left turn to clear the way for the pepper spray. I guess somebody should have told the bad guy the plan because he ran left as well. Both the guys with the foggers followed him and let loose with a volley of pepper spray that would have immobilized the entire Chinese Army - right into my face.

*   *   *

Way back when we used to ride our police motorcycles into the winter. Come about October we took them into the police garage and they would mount sidecars for us. If you know anything about riding motorcycles, you will know that it is completely different trying to steer a motorcycle with a sidecar attached. Normally you just lean over and the bike turns, but with a sidecar you can't lean, so you must steer with the front wheel.

We had our sidecars all mounted, and were getting ready to leave the garage for routine patrol, when one of the fellows admitted he had never ridden a bike with a sidecar before. We gave him a few quick lessons around the garage and he seemed to get the hang of it pretty quickly.

"Right," I said, "follow me," and I headed out into the street, making a smooth left turn. I heard a deafening roar behind me and turned to see my partner shooting across the street at breakneck speed. He was desperately trying

to turn the bike left and was leaning drastically over. The bike, of course, was still going straight and appeared to be accelerating. He crossed six traffic lanes, bounced onto the sidewalk, and mounted the front steps to City Hall. In a resounding crash he drove right into the revolving doors and wedged himself quite firmly there. As he was crashing in, the Mayor was trying to walk out, and the two came face to face. My embarrassed partner looked into the Mayor's face and said, "Your ride is here, sir."

* * *

I loved chewing tobacco. In fact I loved it so much that I chewed constantly on duty and was known to have great wads of the stuff jammed into my cheek at any given time. I had been called to court on a rather serious case and it was my duty at the time to lay out the witness list for the prosecutor so as to allow the evidence to flow chronologically. In doing so I was to be the last witness, and therefore would not be called in the morning, but would be safe until the afternoon session.

The fourth witness had testified and the rest of us were waiting our turns in the witness seclusion area just outside the courtroom. Knowing I had time to kill, I pulled my tobacco pouch from my pocket and tore off a great hunk with my teeth. I tucked it into my cheek and decided it wasn't enough, so I tore off a second great hunk. I could barely close my lips, but I managed to keep it under control. There I was, merrily chomping away, when the court clerk stepped in the room and called me to the stand.

I thought nothing of it and followed her into the courtroom. I took the stand and was sworn in. The clerk looked at me strangely, so I slipped a finger under my belt buckle to check my fly. It was up so I couldn't figure out what was getting her. The prosecutor began asking me questions and I mumbled out the answers as best I could. Finally I noticed a constable at the back of the courtroom waving at me rather discreetly and pointing to his cheek. Suddenly I realized what was wrong; I still had this great wad of tobacco in my cheek.

There was no place to spit and no place to throw out the tobacco, so I did the next best thing I could think of. I swallowed it. Wrong! You don't swallow chewing tobacco. It had hardly hit my stomach when it was on its way back up. I bolted from the stand and fled the courtroom with my hands pressed firmly over my mouth, trying to stem the tide.

I raced into the washroom, let forth the flood, and then proceeded to clean myself up. A short while later I returned to the courtroom, begged the court's forgiveness, and was again placed on the stand. The prosecutor stood up to ask me the next question, and when she made eye contact with me she started to giggle, then chuckle, then roar, and she finally had to sit down. The lawyer joined her, followed by the court clerk, the court recorder and the gallery. I looked at the judge for some help. Up to now he had managed to maintain his composure. When I made eye contact with him he burst forth with such a belly laugh I thought he was going to explode. He had to call a recess, and even when we returned twenty minutes later, the judge was still having trouble composing himself.

CHAPTER TEN

Stories have been coming in from all over the world, a lot of them anonymously and most of them really hilarious. Here is a sampling of a few I received from the Land Down Under (Australia) after circulating some story requests at the 1995 World Police Fire Games. These are alleged to be true!

This is a witness statement received when a man showed up at the hospital with strange burns. The police expected foul play and their investigator returned with this explanation.

"I was watching rugby on the weekend on my telly and had quaffed a few too many ales. My wife was doin' the ironin' beside me, and when she left the room she set the 'ot iron down by the phone. The phone rang an' I grabbed the iron thinkin' it was the phone. 'An that's 'ow I burned my ear."

"How did you burn the other ear?" asked

the investigator.

"I 'adn't anymore than 'ung up when the guy called back!"

This one belongs in the "Believe It Or Not" category.

An ambulance was called to a house and the police responded as well because of the confusing circumstances of the injury. When they arrived, they took a woman aside and asked her for her explanation. This is her statement:

"My husband and I were having a terrific argument this morning at breakfast. I couldn't get my dress zipped up so I stood in front of him for help. He grabbed the zipper and run it up and down so fast he broke it off and we had to cut me out of the dress. I was pissed all day at him at work, and when I came home I saw him lying on his back, working under the car with his legs sticking out. I decided to take revenge and I leaned over and grabbed his fly. I whipped it up and down three or four times, and then went into the kitchen. To my surprise my husband was at the table having an ale so I asked him who was under the car. He told me it was our neighbour and I told him what I had done. We went out to apologize to him but he didn't respond. When we pulled him out we found a

great gash on his forehead from slamming his head into the underside of the car when he got unzipped."

Here is one from a very embarrassed guy who was in the hospital with a broken arm:

"My wife had brought some planters in off our balcony and I guess there was a snake in one of the pots. I was in the bathtub when it decided to leave the planter and slither across the rug in front of my wife. She screamed and I thought someone had broken in and accosted her. I jumped from the tub and ran to help her. I didn't even grab a towel. When I ran into the living room she pointed to the couch and yelled that the snake was under it. I got down on my hands and knees to look for it, and our damn dog came up behind me and cold-nosed me in the ass. I thought it was the snake and I fainted. My wife thought I was having a heart attack and called the ambulance. The medics lifted me onto the stretcher and were just carrying me out when the snake came out from under the couch and scared one of them. He dropped his end of the stretcher and that's when I broke my arm."

Honest! Honest! They tell me these are true! And knowing some of the things that have happened to me I can really believe it. We were called to a cemetery just outside the city limits on an alarm last night, and when we got to the scene we couldn't determine which building the alarm was coming from. My partner dropped me off at the funeral home while he went to check the outbuildings where the equipment was stored. With flashlight in hand I began a check of the perimeter of the building, looking into each window, and half expecting to come face to face with a ghoul or something. I had checked three sides of the building and was just peering into the last room of the funeral parlour, in which there was a body resting peacefully in a casket, when something hit the window beside my face with a loud thwang! My heart stopped and my blood ran cold as every possible scene from every Stephen King movie I ever watched raced through my mind. I turned quickly, with my hand on my gun, and shone my light behind me. Sure enough, there was a bat fluttering away from the building. That was it. I called my partner to come and pick me up right now!

Now that we're on the Tales From the Crypt type stories, here are a few more:

I was walking the beat and it was part of our duty, way back then, to rattle doorknobs and make sure the shopkeepers had remembered to lock their doors before going home at night. I reached for the doorknob at the funeral home, and when I twisted it, the door slid open.

"Great," I thought, "just what I need, a break-in around a bunch of stiffs."

I took out my flashlight and flicked the switch on. I had wanted to remind myself at the beginning of my watch to change the batteries, but I had been distracted and forgot. Now I was about to search a building with a faint yellow light.

I stepped inside and quietly slid the door closed behind me. I moved the dim light around the main room and it was difficult to tell what was what. I walked quietly on the carpet and began checking various rooms. I was becoming more relaxed as I cleared each area and realized that the owner had probably just forgotten to lock up. Nonchalantly, I swung open the door to the last viewing room, and turned my light toward the casket at the back. There was a sudden flurry of movement and a scream.

I damn near fainted. I couldn't find my gun, even though it was still in its holster where it always was, and my voice only squeaked when I tried to say, "Police!"

I staggered back against the wall and found the light switch. I flipped it on and flooded the room with welcome light. There in the middle was the cleaning lady, holding a half eaten sandwich in her hand, her eyes as wide as mine must have been.

"What the hell are you doing?" was the best I could manage to blurt out between heart thumps and gasps for air.

"I'm eating my lunch," she replied through tears.

"Why the hell haven't you got a light on?" I almost yelled back at her.

"I don't like to see the bodies when I eat so I sit in the dark," she said, her voice now quivering.

"Well, for Pete's sake, make some noise or something next time will you," I yelled.

"Okay," she yelled back.

I turned and left the room. Damn, I near had the big one!

Now picture yourself in this police officer's shoes:

There was an alarm at the funeral home, and when we arrived we found an insecure door at the back. K-9 was tied up on a track in another part of the city and backup wasn't available, so we had to clear the building by ourselves. I entered through the open door and was fumbling along the wall for a light switch, when all of a sudden there was a great rustling beside me and something grabbed onto my shoulder through my shirt with claws. It scared the living daylights out of me, of course, and I screamed. My partner started yelling at me to find out what was wrong, and the thing began to scream in my ear. It was all I could do to keep from fainting, and each time I grabbed for the 'thing' it screamed and bit me on the hand. Now it was clawing at my shoulders and biting me on the ear. I was losing it big time!

Finally my partner found the light switch and turned it on. I reached again to my shoulder and grabbed a handful of whatever it was. The creature squawked and flapped as I pulled it away from me and tossed it across the room. It was a damned parrot. The bloody thing had escaped from its cage and triggered the alarm. I could have wrung its neck but I think I had to go back to the station and change my shorts first.

*　　　*　　　*

Watch out Brothers and Sisters, the public has a sense of humour too and sometimes we just set ourselves up for them. They're planting land mines for us and we're stepping on them until there's nothing left but shredded skivvies. Here's another one from a civilian who put a portentous police officer in his

place:

It was a beautiful, mellow, Sunday summer night in September. At about 11:00 P.M. I was returning home from a day at the lake. As I entered the city from the west, a whole string of traffic lights turned green, and there wasn't another vehicle in sight.

Feeling groovy, I put the lead down and went blasting along trying to make as many green lights as possible. The speedometer showed I was going more than forty kilometers per hour over the limit (Okay, American readers, what speed is that?) when a ghost car, parked on a side street, let it all hang out.

I hung a left onto the next street and came to a stop. For some reason, the police officer approached on the passenger side, so I slid over and rolled down the window. The officer proceeded with a stern lecture on speeding and all its consequences.

Finally, he asked, "May I see your pilot's license please?"

Calmly, I reached into my purse and gave it to him. I have held a private pilot's license for some time, a bit of a novelty for a young, good-looking female. As he shone his flashlight onto the document his jaw dropped and an incredulous look spread across his face. For what seemed like minutes, he read and re-read the license in silence. When his speech and composure returned he handed the licence back to me.

"Evening ma'am. Next time watch the speed."

I've often wondered what tale he told his buddies and, although well deserved, I never did get that speeding ticket.

* * *

Guess what! In this, the last chapter of the book, I ran across a stone we had left unturned - Customs!!!! No, no, people you are not going to get away unscathed. The rest of us had to take our medicine, so welcome to the clinic folks. This one arrived from one of your own and it proves that you too are not infallible:

At Customs college, the first and foremost thing we are taught while conducting a personal search on a person is to be professional. Because the person in front of you is going to be stripped down to the skin and vulnerable, we are not supposed to make light of the situation; 'no personal comments, no jokes, no gestures'.

I had been out of college for about a year when my partner and I had the chance to search a car in which we found some marijuana seeds and drug paraphernalia. My partner decided to fill out the paperwork and list the contents of our findings, which left me to conduct the actual search of the subjects. I escorted them into separate rooms and read them the section of the Customs Act which gave us the authority to search. I went into the first room and instructed the subject to take off one piece of clothing at a time and pass it to me. He was down to his underwear when I told him that I wanted him to face the wall, drop his underwear to his knees, and shake them out. He did so. Because he had long hair I required him to shake it out as well before getting dressed.

"Okay," I said to him, "stand up straight and run your hands through your hair."

He stood up straight, turned towards me, and commenced to rub his hands all over his pubic hair.

"That's not what I meant," I said.

* * *

We had a gung-ho type guy in our department who was always getting into stuff off duty. He would follow people in his private vehicle, write down plate numbers, and give them tickets when he came back to work. He hung around drug infested areas on his days off and got involved in off duty arrests and he was generally a pain in the butt to most of us. He was going to get himself hurt one of these times because he didn't have backup.

He lived in a singles only apartment in the downtown core and was a bachelor. One hot summer night, he was resting in bed, naked and not able to sleep. Suddenly he was alerted to the screams of his female next door neighbour. Not wasting a second, he flashed into police mode, grabbed his police issue revolver, flung on his housecoat and raced to the rescue. He stopped for a brief moment outside her apartment door and she again screamed. He knew he must save her! Standing against the far wall he ran at the door, shouldered it, and splintered the lock in one super strike. As he raced through the door, the broken lock caught the tie on his housecoat and tore the garment wide open.

He saw the damsel in distress on the couch, enjoying the last moments of blissful, consentual sex, and screaming as she climaxed. She opened her eyes and spotted a half naked man in her living room pointing and gun at her and her lover. Now she really screamed.

That was the last time he went to a call off duty!

*   *   *

Every now and then a rookie gets his licks in. Okay, okay, I have to be fair and tell

273

you this story. Just remember, rookies, we senior members do your ratings!!

I was barely on the street, the creases were still starched into my shirt, and the graduation spit shine was still on my boots. I was partnered with a senior guy to teach me the ropes and make sure I didn't get myself into trouble until the wetness behind my ears dried a bit. We were working night shift and he instructed me to cruise the industrial area to check property. I no sooner pulled into the first industrial mall and he was snoring. I drove around for a while and then decided I had had enough. I pulled into a business parking lot quickly, slammed on the brakes, hit the overheads and yelled, "He went that way!" pointing to my right. My snoozing partner awoke, bolted from the police vehicle, and ran off around the corner of the building into the darkness. I reached over, closed his door and quietly drove away. I thought he was going to kill me when he got back to the office where I was waiting for him, but he never said a word.

* * *

I went to a bar fight one night, and after the bad guy was in custody I had to take a statement from the victim. I put him into the back of our police car and gave him the appropriate form to fill out. When he completed it I read it over to ensure he had all of the elements necessary to support the charge of assault. About half way through the statement I saw something like this, "!@%&***%$$$#!"

"What the hell is this?" I asked, pointing to the scribbles.

"Oh, that's where the guy started swearing at me," he replied.

I shook my head and kept on reading. A few lines later I saw something like this, "**✧****☆* !" I pointed to the line and again asked, "and this?"

"Well, what do you think, that's where I pissed the guy off enough that he hit me with a bat and I saw stars!"

*   *   *

We were dispatched to a break and enter residential in progress. The guy on the phone had called 9-1-1 and was whispering that someone was in his house right now. As we arrived we observed a male climbing down a ladder at the rear of the house and immediately took him into custody. We were taking him to the police car when the victim came out of the house and looked at the guy in cuffs.

"David?" he said with astonishment.

"You know this guy?" I asked.

"He's my brother!" the victim replied.

Just then the victim's wife came out in her housecoat and stood silently on the steps.

"I think the three of you better talk," I said, taking the handcuffs off the brother.

*　　　*　　　*

One early morning a releasee from the drunk tank discovered a police car in the alley behind the police station with the keys in it. Not seeing anyone in the area he decided that this would be fun and he would take the car for a drive, maybe even play with all the buttons. He hopped inside, started it up and drove away.

Shortly thereafter, the two officers who were supposed to have the vehicle, came to the back alley and discovered that their car was gone. At first they thought it was a prank, but when they heard a drunken voice singing over their portable radios, their worst nightmare was realized. They ran up to dispatch and told the sergeant what had happened. The dispatcher tried in vain for about half an hour to get the drunk to pull over. He refused and kept singing. Every car in the city was alerted, but somehow the guy managed to avoid them.

About 0600 hours the radio crackled to life again and the drunk was on the air.

"Bad guy to gas truck, bad guy to gas

truck," he slurred.

The dispatcher seized the opportunity, "Gas truck to bad guy, what do you need?"

"I'm outta gas at the corner of Smith and Jones Streets," he replied.

"Not a problem," she said, "you wait right there and I'll be over to fix you up."

In seconds about twenty police cars descended on the unsuspecting drunk.

*   *   *

I was sent to a late night neighbour dispute, and when I arrived I found the complainant sitting at his fire pit in the back yard. An empty case of beer sat beside him, and it soon became obvious that he had consumed the entire thing himself. He started to tell us about an argument he had been having with his neighbour when I noticed that he had hfeet on the rim of the fire pit and his runners were starting to smoke.

I tapped him on the shoulder and he said, "No, no, let me finish, let me finish."

I said, "Okay," and continued to watch his smoking sneakers.

He rambled on and on as I watched the bottom of his runners begin to melt. He was so pissed he didn't even feel it. I tapped him on the shoulder again.

"Are you going to let me finish, or are

you going to keep interrupting?" he yelled at me.

I folded my arms, sighed, and stood back while he completed his tale of woe.

Finally the sneakers reached the flash point and they burst into flames.

"Holy shit!" he yelled, jumping to his feet and stomping on the freshly mowed grass. Each time he hit the ground with his foot, the melting rubber picked up a glob of cut grass, and by the time he got the flames out he had about three inches of grass on each foot.

Not missing a beat he smothered the flames and continued with his story. He never responded to the burn, and when I asked him if he wanted an ambulance, he had no idea why I would ask him that. I would hate to be him in the morning.

*   *   *

DUMB CRIMINAL ALERT!!!!

A first-time bank robber struck a small branch in a crowded downtown area. He did not produce a gun, but told the teller that he had one, and she obliged by giving him the contents of the cash drawer. The thief grabbed the cash and ran out the door. He was about a block away when he was suddenly confronted by another thief with a real gun, who promptly relieved him of his day's earnings and fled. The first bad guy went immediately to a payphone and dialed 9-1-1 to report that he had been robbed. He then waited for police to arrive so he could fill in his report. Needless to say the police took no time at all to match his description to the bank robber.

*　　*　　*

DUMBER CRIMINAL ALERT!!!!!

I was driving behind a car on a side street one night only because we happened to be going the same direction. There were two bodies in the car and they were watching me, thinking that I was paying attention to them. I really had no interest in them whatsoever. Without warning, the car pulled to the side of the road, the occupants got out and put their hands on the roof and waited. I turned on the overheads and pulled in behind them, thinking they may be lost or having some car trouble.

As I stepped from the police car the driver said, "Yeah, you're right, I'm a suspended driver, this car is stolen and it don't got no insurance on it!"

Of course, I immediately placed them both under arrest and thanked them for their cooperation.

*   *   *

Our city is expanding and land is continually being annexed farther and farther out which gives us more and more country area to patrol. We had been policing an area of large rolling hills to the west of the city for a few months and there was nothing there but fields and old bales of hay. It made a great place for us to come and play bumper tag on night shift.

We just returned from five days off and had a bit of piss n' vinegar in us on our first night shift. About three in the morning we decided to make a meet with another car crew and play some tag in the field. The week before, we found a large hill on the south end of one of the pastures that completely hid the police car when we drove behind it. We figured this would be a good place to hide and we could sneak up on the other crew when they arrived.

Off we headed to the field in the dead of night, and when we reached the pasture, we headed directly for the hill on the south side. My partner, who was driving, decided that we could get on top of the hill and wait until we saw the other car crew's headlights. Once we knew they were approaching, we could slide down the back of the hill and hide on them. Good plan!

We headed up to the top of the hill with

confidence and a little speed, and were almost at the crest when the car suddenly dropped out from under us. We went straight down about thirty feet and landed with a bang. Everything in the inside of the car went flying, our hats, jackets, the briefcase (which was open of course), flashlights, summons book, and us. I flew up and struck my head on the roof and my partner went forward and split his lip open on the steering wheel. As I came down I lunged forward and caught the bottom of my chin on the shotgun in the rack. The lights went out and I think I actually heard little birdies.

When I came to, I shook my pounding head trying to clear it.

My partner was looking around in a bit of a stupor. "I think they started construction while we were on days off," he observed.

"No shit," I replied.

Just then the other car crew arrived and located us in the carved out ravine.

"You guys okay?" they asked.

"Yup," I called back, "a few scrapes and our car is bent, but we're okay."

"Good," said the driver, and tapped the front of our car with his bumper, "You're it!" and they left.

*   *   *

"City Police, can I help you?"

"I heard if I win the lottery I'm gonna be a stinking devil."

"Well then you might consider taking a shower at least."

"No way! I don't want and don't like showers!!!"

"So you'd rather be a stinking devil than a nice clean one who can go out and have lots of fun?"

"What? I don't want to talk to you anymore, you're trying to persuade me to go the other way!"

Click.

EPILOGUE

Well folks, bdya, bdya, bdya, that's all for now. I've had an absolute scream working on this second book. This is funnier than a fart in a space suit. Speaking of things in space, we recently had two detectives from a small western city arrive at our police club on a trip to Las Vegas. They were stopping over and wanted to meet a few of our members. Well, they met a few of the ones who can really put away the firewater, and as a result they passed out about 0400 hours (you should know the time by now). Their drinking partners wanted to make sure they didn't miss their plane to Vegas in the morning, so they called for a paddy wagon to pick these two up and drop them off at the airport.

The paddy wagon arrived and the detectives were poured into the back. They were driven to the airport and the nice policemen even carried them into the ticket area and got them booked onto a flight. Around noon the two detectives were being awakened by airline staff.

"Are we in Vegas?" one of them asked, trying to strip the fur from his tongue.

"No, you're in Regina, Saskatchewan."

"How the hell did we get here?"

"Don't ask me, you're the detective."

Our guys swear they took them through the international gate and got them seated in the loading area for the flight to Vegas.

Being a police officer has definitely been a very different vocation. As you can tell from having read this book (and the first one TALES FROM THE POLICE LOCKER ROOM) there is a lighter side to the career. No, hell, it's damned funny. How funny is it?

* * *

"City Police, how can I help you?"

"I want to report robbery!"

"Okay, tell me what happened."

"I call from Nuclear Sub Shop, man come in and order three subs, then he run away and not pay me!"

"How long ago did this happen, sir?"

"Right now! He just run out door!"

"What is the description, sir?"

"One chicken sub on brown, one meatball sub on white and one salami sub on white."

*   *   *

A young man decided to augment his income by doing a little purse snatching in the local park. Not being very fleet of foot he decided that the best way to make good his escape was to use his bicycle. He rode to the park, and after making one complete circle of the grassy area, saw a lady with a purse walking all by herself. He raced up behind her and grabbed the sling on her purse as he flew past. The purse came away easily and he thrilled at the fact that his first attempt at criminal activity had been so easy and so successful.

When he arrived home with the purse hidden under his jacket, there were the police waiting for him and there was the lady victim from the park - his own mother!

*   *   *

I was interviewing the teenage victim of a robbery in the emergency room of the hospital. He had been stabbed in the throat and robbed of a small amount of money at a store. The bad guy had run outside and was confronted by a group of men who were entering the store. He ran from them but one of the guys picked up a rock and flung it at him. He struck the bad guy in the back of the head but the thief still managed to make good his escape.

"And could you recognize this robber if you saw him again?" I asked the victim.

Just then an ambulance crew arrived with a new patient and flung back the curtains to drop off a victim with a pretty good gash on the back of his head.

My victim leaned over and pointed at the new arrival.

"That's him right there!" he said.

We made our arrest immediately. It's not often the bad guy is brought right to you.

*　　*　　*

We were on a stakeout and hadn't had a break since 1800 hours. We were parked in the dark in an alley watching a vehicle which was supposed to be loaded with drugs. Suddenly we realized we were very, very hungry. I sent the following CAD message to the dispatcher on our computer:

"To DW29: Please contact nearest pizza place to our location and order one large special with everything and two Cokes. My credit card number is 5432-1234-9876. Tell the delivery guy to come down the back alley from the east with his lights off and we are sitting in the car behind the sixth house from the east end."

In about twenty minutes we saw a dark car enter the alley, drive slowly towards us, and then stop. We heard some scuffling and I saw a hand come up over my window sill.

The pizza guy, in his little hat and apron, whispered, "Did you guys order a pizza?"

"Yeah, we did," I whispered back.

"Okay be right back," he whispered and dropped to the ground again.

I looked in the rearview mirror, and in a few minutes I saw the pizza guy coming back towards our car, doing a duck-walk with the pizza box above his head in one hand and two Cokes in the other. When he pulled up beside our car all I could see was the pizza box.

"Here, you go," he whispered.

I took the box and the Cokes and thanked him very much.

I watched in the mirror as he duck-walked away.

Well at least we were going to be able to eat. I tossed the pizza up onto the dash and we ripped the top of the box. In a matter of seconds the front window was so steamed up we couldn't see out of it. Maybe this wasn't such a good idea after all!

I leave you with this last tale for now and bid you 10-8 (that means 'clear and available') 'till next time.

*   *   *

Statement taken from a victim of an armed robbery at a gas station:

It was about 2:00 A.M. when this guy came into the gas bar and tossed a twenty dollar bill on the counter. He asked for change and when I opened the till he pulled a knife on me. He said, "Give me everything in the till." So I did. I gave him all the cash that was in there and he ran away leaving the twenty dollar bill on the counter. There was only fifteen dollars in the till so I guess I'm ahead five bucks.

Keep smiling, and the next time you see a police car, remember some of the tales from this book. They won't know what you're laughing at.

The Odessy Continues!

I would like you to be a part of the next book.

I'm not stopping here! I'm already compiling stories for the next book in the series and I want to offer you the opportunity to be a part of it. I will be attaching a **donor** page in the next issue and it will contain the names of those who have submitted stories and wish to be recognized. But, if you want to remain anonymous, that's no problem either. Send your stories, photos and/or tapes to:

Wordstorm Productions Inc.,
P.O. Box 49132, 7740 - 18 Street S.E.,
Calgary, Alberta, Canada
T2C 3W5
e-mail: wordstrm@cadvision.com
or
in the United States send to
Wordstorm Productions Inc.,
1520 - 3rd St NW, C104,
Great Falls MT, USA 59404

ORDERING INFORMATION

Tales from the Police Locker room
Vols. I & II
make excellent gifts for anyone.

To order in Canada please send cheque
or money order in Canadian funds to:

WORDSTORM PRODUCTIONS INC.
PO BOX 49132, 7740 - 18 ST. SE,
CALGARY, ALBERTA, CANADA T2C 3W5

$9.95 + $3.00 (shipping and handling) + $.91 (GST)
= $13.86

To order in the United States please
send cheque or money order in US funds
to:

WORDSTORM PRODUCTIONS INC.,
1520 - 3 ST NW, C-104,
GREAT FALLS, MONTANA, USA
59404

$9.95 + $3.50 (shipping and handling)
= $13.45

About the Author

Perry began seeking a serious writing career in 1980 with the production of a fantasy novel called "The Sword." The book remains unpublished but served as the launching pad for Perry. Throughout the years following he honed his skill and explored various markets. He tried his hand at freelancing for magazines, editing newsletters and producing a new art form called "Rose Prose."

1993 saw the launcing of TALES FROM THE POLICE LOCKER ROOM VOL. I and Perry's first forray into the world of self publishing. After receiving nearly fifty rejection slips from publishers he successfully entered the market. As a result he formed his own publishing company, WORDSTORM PRODUCTIONS INC.